PHILIP ALLAN

LITERATURE GUIDE

FOR GCSE

TO KILL A MOCKINGBIRD
HARPER LEE

Susan Elkin

With thanks to Jeanette Weatherall for reviewing the manuscript of this book

Philip Allan Updates, an imprint of Hodder Education, an Hachette UK company,
Market Place, Deddington, Oxfordshire OX15 0SE

Orders

Bookpoint Ltd, 130 Milton Park, Abingdon, Oxfordshire OX14 4SB
tel: 01235 827720
fax: 01235 400454
e-mail: uk.orders@bookpoint.co.uk
Lines are open 9.00 a.m.–5.00 p.m., Monday to Saturday, with a 24-hour message
answering service. You can also order through the Philip Allan Updates website:
www.philipallan.co.uk

© Philip Allan Updates 2010
ISBN 978-1-4441-1022-7
First printed 2010

Impression number 5 4 3 2 1
Year 2015 2014 2013 2012 2011 2010

Printed in Spain

Hachette UK's policy is to use papers that are natural, renewable and recyclable products and
made from wood grown in sustainable forests. The logging and manufacturing processes are
expected to conform to the environmental regulations of the country of origin.

Contents

Introduction

How to use this guide

You may find it useful to read sections of this guide when you need them, rather than reading it from start to finish. For example, you may find it helpful to read the *Plot and structure* section in conjunction with the novel or the *Context* section before you start reading the novel. The sections relating to assessments will be especially useful in the weeks leading up to the exam.

The following features have been used throughout this guide:

- A list of **introductory questions** to target your thinking is provided at the beginning of each chapter. Look back at these once you have read the chapter and check you have understood each of them before you move on.

- What are the novel's main themes?

- Pay particular attention to the **Grade booster** boxes. Students with a firm grasp of these ideas are likely to be aiming for the top grades.

Grade *booster*

- Broaden your thinking about the text by answering the questions in the **Pause for thought** boxes. They are intended to encourage you to consider your own opinions in order to develop your skills of criticism and analysis.

Pause for thought

- **Key quotations** are highlighted for you, and you may wish to use these as evidence in your examination answers. Because there are so many editions of this text, chapter numbers rather than page numbers have been used to locate quotations from the text.

Key quotation

'I think there's just one kind of folks. Folks.'
(Scout, Chapter 23)

- Use the **Text focus** boxes to practise evaluating the text in detail and looking for evidence to support your understanding.

Text **focus**

- The **Grade focus** sections explain how you may be assessed and distinguish between higher and foundation responses.

Grade *focus*

- Use the **Review your learning** sections to test your knowledge after you have read each chapter.

Review your learning

- Don't forget to go online for further self-tests on the text:
www.philipallan.co.uk/literatureguidesonline

How to approach the text

A novel is, above all, a narrative. A large part of the storyteller's art is to make you want to find out what happens next, and to keep you reading to the end. In order to study *To Kill a Mockingbird,* and to enjoy it, you need to keep a close track of the events that take place. This guide will help you to do that, but you may also benefit from keeping your own notes about the main events and who is involved in them.

However, any novel consists of much more than its events. Although you need to know the story well to get a good grade in your GCSE exam, if you spend a lot of time simply retelling the story you will not get a high mark. You must be aware of a number of other features:

- You need to consider the **setting** of the novel — where the events take place — and how this influences the story.
- You need to get to know the **characters** and how the author, Harper Lee, tells us what they are like. Consider what they say and do, and what other people say about them. Also think about why they behave in the way they do — their motives — and what clues the author gives us about this.
- As you read on, you will also notice **themes** — the ideas explored by the author. You may find it easier to think about these while not actually reading the book, especially if you discuss them with other people.
- You should also try to become aware of the **style** of the novel, especially on a second reading — this means *how* the author tells the story.
- The elements above are all dealt with in this guide. However, you should always try to notice them for yourself. This guide is no substitute for a careful and thoughtful reading of the text.

Watching the film

In 1962, two years after the publication of the book, Universal Studios made a black-and-white film of *To Kill a Mockingbird*, directed by Robert Mulligan. Harper Lee's novel had already won the Pulitzer Prize for Fiction — an award given annually for fiction by an American author — and the actor Gregory Peck won a Best Actor Oscar for his performance as Atticus Finch in the film.

It is a fine film and in many ways true to the text. Mary Badham's portrayal of Scout is very faithful to the textual character. Harper Lee is said to have been so overcome by Peck's likeness to her father that she afterwards gave him her father's watch as a thank-you gift and keepsake. Set designers travelled to Monroeville (see page 5) and made an almost exact replica of the county courthouse for the trial scene. So it is clear that a great deal of attention was paid to detail.

However, when you are studying a novel for an exam, films (and plays) based on the book have to be treated with caution. A film can only ever be *based* on a novel. There are bound to be changes because what works on the printed page does not always work in a visual medium.

For example, how could Scout's first-person narrative be conveyed on screen? Although the film uses a certain amount of voice-over to communicate this, for much of the time you simply see the children doing things and lose sight of the fact that the story is told by Scout. This is particularly apparent when, in the film, Scout goes with Jem, Calpurnia and Atticus to tell Helen Robinson that her husband Tom has been killed. In the novel, Scout stays at home and Dill tells her about it afterwards. Examiners are unimpressed by students who refer to the film rather than the text, and it is easy to make a mistake with this sort of detail if you have seen the film several times but read the novel only casually. Similarly, in the novel Atticus tells Scout that he has been asked by Judge Taylor to defend Tom. We do not 'see' the actual conversation. However, in the film the judge calls on Atticus and chats to him about it on his veranda.

Then there is the question of length. *To Kill a Mockingbird* is more than 300 pages long. The film runs for just over two hours. Inevitably, the director Robert Mulligan and the screenplay writer had to cut the plot drastically. This means that many details, characters and incidents, which you need to know about when studying the novel, are missing from the film. They include:

- the burning of Miss Maudie's house
- Aunt Alexandra
- the visit to First Purchase Church
- Mrs Dubose
- Link Deas
- Dolphus Raymond

Pause for thought

By 1962, films were usually made in colour. Why do you think Universal Studios chose to make *To Kill a Mockingbird* in black and white?

If you see the film and get too familiar with it before you have studied the text in depth, the film's strong visual messages can easily block out your memory of what is in the novel. It is therefore better to watch the film only after you have got to know the novel well. Then you can view it critically (and enjoyably) and work out for yourself why Mulligan made some of the decisions he did. Used in that way, the film will probably help with your understanding of the story. Do not watch the

film as part of your last-minute revision, however, because it will blur your memory of what is in the novel and what is not.

There is also a play version of *To Kill a Mockingbird* adapted for the stage by Christopher Sergel.

Pause for thought

If you want to study the film in greater depth (perhaps because you plan to take film studies at A-level), see the interesting and useful book *Screen Adaptations: Harper Lee's To Kill a Mockingbird* by R. Barton Palmer (Methuen Drama, 2008). It studies the relationship between the text and the film.

Context

- **What is Harper Lee's background?**
- **Are her characters based on real people?**
- **What is the history of black people in the American South?**
- **Why were people particularly poor in the 1930s?**
- **What inspired Harper Lee to write the novel in the late 1950s?**
- **How does *To Kill a Mockingbird* relate to other fiction from the Southern states?**

Fact and fiction

Harper Lee was born in Monroeville, Alabama, in 1926. She was the youngest of four children and her father was a lawyer.

Jean Louise ('Scout') Finch, the narrator of *To Kill a Mockingbird*, was born in the same year as her creator in a fictional Alabama town called Maycomb. Scout's father, Atticus, is a lawyer and she is the younger child in the family.

To Kill a Mockingbird is a good example of fiction that has developed from the author's personal experiences. Maycomb is based on Monroeville and Atticus is based on Harper Lee's own father.

Harper Lee in the Monroeville Courthouse, 1961

Pause for thought

Can you think of other books you may have read in which the author's own life story is partly woven into the fiction? *Anita and Me* by Meera Syal, *David Copperfield* by Charles Dickens, *Jane Eyre* by Charlotte Brontë, *The Kite Runner* by Khaled Hosseini and *Carrie's War* by Nina Bawden are all examples.

The character of Scout is probably much like the young Harper Lee. The author has freely admitted that she based the character of Dill on Truman Capote, another American novelist who grew up in Monroeville and was a childhood friend.

Many of the places mentioned in the novel, such as Mobile, and the state capital Montgomery, are real. *The Mobile Register*, which Scout was 'born reading', and Atticus's favourite *Montgomery Advertiser*, are real newspapers still published today.

Harper Lee studied law at Alabama State University. A few months after graduating in 1950, she left for New York. She worked as a reservation clerk at an airline for a few years before giving up her job to develop a full-time career as a writer.

Slavery

To make sense of *To Kill a Mockingbird*, you need to understand the history of Alabama and the other Southern states.

Alabama, formerly an independent state, signed up to become part of the USA in 1819. In the late 1700s and early 1800s, the Southern states had a thriving economy based on the production of cotton and other valuable crops like sugar and rice. Plantations (large farms) were owned by rich white families who ran their businesses by using hundreds of black slaves as their labour force.

These black people, or their ancestors, had been forcibly transported to the Caribbean and to the USA from Africa on the notorious slave ships. Many of the ships involved were owned by British traders who made large profits out of this 'cargo' until slave trading was made illegal in Britain in 1807.

In the Southern states, the slaves picked and processed the crops and did all the menial jobs. They lived in basic accommodation provided on-site by the plantation owner. They were slaves and therefore not free to leave. Only if they were sold did they move. They were not paid for their work but food was provided. A few lucky individuals worked in their owners' homes as domestic servants such as cooks, cleaners and carers of children. These slaves usually lived in a building close to the house or sometimes in servants' rooms within the house.

This system meant that white landowners could afford to live elegantly in large houses. Before 1861, there was a distinctive leisurely, aristocratic lifestyle among slave owners in the unindustrialised Southern states.

Life was different in the industrialised North of the country. Northerners objected to what they saw as the exploitation of black people by their fellow Americans in the South, which, incidentally, gave the South an 'unfair' advantage over the North commercially. Therefore, those in the North campaigned for the abolition of slavery.

The result was that the Southern states, including Alabama, tried to secede (break away) from the Union. They wanted to form a new country called the Confederate States of America. This led to a civil war between the Northern (Union) states and the Southern (Confederate) states, fought on the issue of slavery, between 1861 and 1865.

The Confederates lost the war. Slavery was then outlawed immediately by the Emancipation Proclamation. In practice, however, most slaves continued to work for their former owners on the same plantations and the notion of equal status was a short-lived ideal.

Black people continued to be treated as inferior, made to live separately from whites and were denied their rights. They were free in name only for almost another century. *To Kill a Mockingbird* shows blacks, like the Robinsons and the congregation of Calpurnia's church, living apart from the white community and with a poor standard of living 70 years after the Civil War.

Grade *booster*

As a revision or note-making exercise construct a map of Maycomb as you read and re-read the novel. It will help you to get your understanding of the plot absolutely clear.

Black workers gather the cotton harvest in Louisiana

TopFoto

The 1930s

The Wall Street Crash of 1929, in which many company shares became worthless overnight, led to a period of poverty and high unemployment throughout the USA and Europe. Wall Street is the street in New York in and around which banks and financial institutions are clustered. It is the equivalent of the City district of London.

The situation was worst between 1933 and 1935 when hundreds of businesses collapsed and millions lost their jobs. This time is known as the Great Depression and Harper Lee, like her creation Scout Finch, grew up

Desperate times followed the Wall Street Crash of October 1929

Key quotation

'The Cunninghams are country folks, farmers, and the crash hit them hardest.'

(Atticus, Chapter 2)

Key quotation

Atticus said professional people were poor because the farmers were poor. As Maycomb County was farm country, nickels and dimes were hard to come by for doctors and dentists and lawyers.

(Scout, Chapter 2)

during this period. In *To Kill a Mockingbird* the (white) Cunninghams and Ewells, and most of the black people, are poor partly because of the Depression.

The 1930s was a decade of change. In 1931, when Harper Lee was five years old, nine young black men were arrested in Scottsboro, Alabama and tried for the rape of two white women. Just as Tom Robinson is threatened by a lynch mob in *To Kill a Mockingbird*, these men came close to being killed by a vigilante group before trial. Although medical evidence proved that the women had not been raped, all the defendants were found guilty by the all-white jury. They were sentenced to death apart from the youngest, aged only 12. After a series of appeals and retrials, they were eventually proved to be innocent and all but one of them was freed or granted parole.

The miscarriage of justice at Scottsboro, and other similar trials in which people were judged by their colour and not on the facts, obviously influenced Harper Lee. It is not hard to see why she included Tom Robinson's trial as the climax of the plot of *To Kill a Mockingbird*. Her novel is really about the attempt of one man, Atticus Finch, to make his community recognise that black people are full human beings entitled to equal rights.

Pause for thought

What does *To Kill a Mockingbird* teach you about how the Wall Street Crash affected the everyday lives of ordinary Americans?

The 1950s and 1960s

During the 1950s, towns in Alabama and elsewhere in the Southern states were insular and isolated. Racial tension still dominated. Harper Lee, who has always divided her time between Monroeville and New York, would have been well aware of this. Scout describes Maycomb as 'a tired old

town' for whose inhabitants there is 'nothing to see outside the boundaries of Maycomb County'.

By 1954, Martin Luther King Junior was working as a Baptist church minister in Montgomery, the state capital, and his civil rights work began there. He worked to bring an end to prejudice and segregation, and to ensure voting rights for black people.

In 1955, Rosa Parks, a black woman, refused to give up her seat to a white man on a bus in Montgomery, leading to a bus boycott by black people that eventually forced the end of segregated public transport. Harper Lee would have been writing her novel at this time. However, it was not until after Martin Luther King Junior's assassination in 1968 that, at last, his life's aims began to be fulfilled.

Martin Luther King Jnr speaking at a mass rally in Philadelphia

To Kill a Mockingbird was first published in 1960. It had been reviewed by a publisher three years before in 1957 and then substantially redrafted. It has since sold over 30 million copies worldwide and has won numerous awards, including the Pulitzer Prize. It remains Harper Lee's only novel, although she has written magazine articles and essays. In 1962, it was made into a successful film starring Gregory Peck as Atticus, a performance for which he won an Oscar.

A Southern novel

The Southern states had — and still have — a clear identity of their own. It is possible that this identity was formed or strengthened by their defeat in the American Civil War.

'Southern novels' (novels written by American authors from the South) tend to be regional and to present a strong sense of place. They also convey a feeling of loneliness and isolation. Notice the way Harper Lee describes the layout of Maycomb in such detail that the reader knows where each place is in relation to the rest of the town.

After the Civil War, the Southern states went into a long decline and were, in some ways, cut off from the progressive North. Poverty was worse in the South during the Depression than in the North because farming, on which the South depended, was badly affected.

Although many Southerners moved to the North, this was prompted by, and led to, ambivalent feelings. The migrants suffered homesickness and nostalgia and regretted the passing of the old Southern traditions. On the other hand, many of them hated the Southern values that had driven them North in the first place. In *To Kill a Mockingbird,* for example, Dolphus Raymond sends his 'mixed' children to the North where they will not stand out as being different.

The courthouse in Monroeville

You can see this ambivalence clearly in the novel. Harper Lee recognises that there is much that is wrong with Maycomb, but she also presents a certain affection for its ways. There is gentle exasperation in telling the reader that 'Maycomb was interested by the news of Tom's death for perhaps two days'.

White Southerners are proud of their aristocratic heritage — look at the discussions about 'fine folks' in *To Kill a Mockingbird* and at the views of Aunt Alexandra (Chapter 13). On the other hand, there is a sense of guilt. Many Maycomb inhabitants are still living mentally in the age of slavery, but characters like Atticus, Miss Maudie and Calpurnia are beginning to prick at other people's consciences. Like many Southern novelists, Harper Lee expresses pride in the South's history alongside shame at its racism.

Violence, often directed at black people, is also typical of Southern novels. The party of Old Sarum men coming in the night to confront the jailed Tom Robinson is firmly in this tradition.

Southern values mean that, however bad things are, you must defend your honour. The Ewells live on a rubbish dump and are, in a sense, worse off than anyone else in the novel. Bob Ewell is a violent liar who lives on state benefits and spends all his money on drink, but he is determined to protect his 'honour'. This attitude is partly rooted in fear. After the abolition of slavery, some white people were afraid they would lose not only land and money but also status.

Grade *booster*

Work out what you understand by the term 'Southern values'. Once your understanding is clear use the term, where appropriate, in your essays because it will show that you understand not only the novel's plot and 'message' but also its very specific context.

> ### Review your learning
> 1 Where, when and how did Harper Lee grow up?
> 2 Why was a civil war fought in the USA?
> 3 Who led the US campaign for equal rights for black people in the 1950s and 1960s?
> 4 What do Southern novels tend to have in common?
> 5 In view of what you know about Harper Lee's background, why do you think she wrote *To Kill a Mockingbird*?
> 6 Why do you think *To Kill a Mockingbird* has been such a successful novel, with high sales worldwide?
>
> **More interactive questions and answers online.**

Plot and structure

- **What happens in each chapter?**
- **How is the timing of events in the novel worked out?**
- **What is the overall 'shape' of the novel?**
- **How does Harper Lee organise her material to keep the reader interested?**

Plot

Part One

Chapter 1

- Members of the Finch family and their background.
- Charlie Baker Harris (Dill) staying next door with Miss Rachel Haverford for the summer.
- First mention of Boo Radley.

Atticus Finch is a widowed lawyer bringing up two children, Jean Louise ('Scout') aged six — who is telling the story — and Jeremy ('Jem') aged 12 in Maycomb. He is helped by Calpurnia, a respected black cook, house-keeper and substitute mother. The children make friends with Charles Baker ('Dill') Harris from Mississippi who is spending the summer with his aunt. All three children are fascinated by the unseen Arthur ('Boo') Radley, a neighbour.

Chapter 2

- Dill leaves Maycomb.
- Scout's first morning at school.
- Miss Caroline Fisher's disappointing teaching.
- Walter Cunningham's poverty.

Scout misses Dill and finds school disappointing because her young teacher, who is new to the school, disapproves of her ability to read. Then a misunderstanding arises when Scout tries to explain to Miss Caroline that Walter Cunningham has brought neither packed lunch nor money to school because he is poor. Scout knows the family because, in the previous year, Atticus had done legal work for Walter's father for which

Mr Cunningham could pay Atticus only 'in kind' by bringing, for example, logs and hickory nuts for the Finch family.

Text **focus**

Look carefully at Chapter 2 from 'My special knowledge of the Cunningham tribe' to 'Jem's definitions are very nearly accurate sometimes'. Read it several times.

- Note that Jem tells Scout that an entailment is 'a condition of having your tail in a crack'. This is an example of one of Harper Lee's many wry jokes, this time at Jem's expense. It is an instance of **irony**. Jem has invented the definition. An entailment is actually a legal term meaning that there is a limitation on what an owner may do with his property. However, can you see what Atticus means when he says 'Jem's definitions are very nearly accurate sometimes'? Mr Cunningham cannot do what he wants to because of the entailment — like an animal whose tail is trapped. That is what makes Jem's definition ironic.

- There is evidence in this passage of the poverty that the working people in Maycomb experience and the reaction of professional people such as lawyers and doctors to it. They will accept goods such as logs, nuts, holly or potatoes as payment for services instead of money. Such bartering of goods and services helps everyone in difficult times because poverty caused by an economic depression affects all classes. Atticus tells Scout, 'We are indeed' when she asks him whether their own family is poor.

- Harper Lee often uses short sentences with one subject and one verb, such as 'We watched', 'Jem's nose wrinkled' and 'Entailment was only part of Mr Cunningham's vexations'. The technical name for this is a **simple sentence** (as opposed to a **compound** or **complex sentence**). The frequency of simple sentences makes the writing direct and incisive. It is an appropriate style for a story about children growing up. Find other examples of simple sentences in this passage and think about their effect.

- Look carefully at the way Harper Lee sets out the dialogue in this passage. She makes it move quickly by omitting 'he said', 'she said' or their equivalents. It is a technique borrowed from drama and perhaps it is not surprising that the novel has been made into a successful film and a play for live performance. Lee's style of writing conversations already reads rather like a play script.

- Earlier in this chapter, Scout says, 'He hasn't taught me anything, Miss Caroline. Atticus ain't got time to teach me anything.' What evidence can you find here that shows this is untrue?

- What is the evidence that the Cunninghams are a 'set breed of men'?

Chapter 3

- Walter Cunningham has lunch with the Finches.
- Calpurnia rebukes Scout for bad manners.
- First mention of Ewell family through Burris — who is both dirty and rude at school.
- Scout and Atticus discuss school.

Jem invites Walter Cunningham home for lunch but Scout angers Calpurnia by commenting tactlessly on Walter's eating habits. In the afternoon, Miss

Caroline is upset by lice-infested Burris Ewell, who storms abusively out of school. Later Scout tells Atticus that she does not want to go to school. Atticus explains sympathetically that she must but he promises to go on reading with her despite the teacher's instructions.

Chapter 4

- Gifts found in a tree on Radley property.
- Dill returns for summer 1934.
- Atticus questions the children about their make-believe games.
- Radleys heard laughing.

Scout finds some wrapped chewing gum left for her in an oak tree near the Radley house. Later, she and Jem find old coins there. With Dill, they begin to develop a make-believe game based on local rumours and legends about Boo Radley. Atticus catches them and suspects they are planning to torment Boo. Scout thinks she hears laughter in the Radley house when she unintentionally gets close to it by rolling inside a tyre.

Chapter 5

- Miss Maudie explains Boo Radley's background.
- Children try to force Boo Radley outside.
- Atticus forbids them to play 'One Man's Family'.

Miss Maudie Atkinson is a sensible, humane neighbour who dislikes gossip. She tells Scout that Boo is a shy, damaged man bullied by his late father, who just wants to stay indoors. The next day the three children try to entice Boo Radley out of his house. Atticus discovers them and stops the game, forbidding them to play the Boo Radley-based make-believe game in future.

Chapter 6

- The children approach the Radley house in the dark.
- Nathan Radley shoots but misses them.
- Jem's trousers are left behind.

The children dare each other to sneak onto the Radley veranda in the dark. Boo's elder brother, Nathan, mistakes them for a black burglar and shoots. In the panic as they run way, Jem catches his trousers on a wire fence and leaves them. Neighbours hear the noise and come to investigate. Later that night when the commotion has died down Jem retrieves the trousers.

Chapter 7

- Jem's trousers mysteriously already mended when he takes them back.
- More gifts in the tree.
- Nathan Radley blocks hole in the tree where gifts were left.

Jem tells Scout that when he went back to the Radley house, his trousers had been mended and deliberately left on the top of the fence for him to collect. In the hole in the oak tree the children find various gifts over several weeks. Soon they discover the hole has been filled with cement by Nathan Radley who says it is because the tree is dying. Actually, it is to stop his brother leaving things for the children.

Chapter 8

- Mrs Radley dies.
- Snowfall in Maycomb — very unusual.
- The children build a snowman.
- Miss Maudie's house burns.

Nathan and Boo's rarely seen mother dies during the winter 'of natural causes' but nobody takes much notice. Scout is disconcerted by her first sight of snow. Then the children build a snow model of their fat neighbour, Mr Avery. During the night, Miss Maudie's house accidentally catches fire and is destroyed, but she shows great courage in accepting the loss. Someone — she does not realise who — quietly puts a blanket around Scout's shoulders while she is watching the fire.

Chapter 9

- Atticus to defend a black man accused of rape.
- Scout already taunted at school about her father's tolerance of black people.
- Christmas at Aunt Alexandra's home.
- Scout fights her second cousin Francis.
- Uncle Jack disciplines Scout.
- Conversation between Atticus and Uncle Jack.

Cecil Jacobs taunts Scout whose 'daddy defended niggers'. Atticus later explains that he intends to defend Tom Robinson, a black man accused of rape. Meanwhile, the children and Atticus spend Christmas with Aunt Alexandra, sister to Atticus and Jack. Her grandson Francis, Scout's second cousin, goads Scout about her 'nigger-lover' father so they fight. Uncle

Jack, a doctor, punishes her for fighting and for her abusive language but apologises when he learns what the fight was about. Scout later overhears — as she is meant to — Atticus telling Jack that he hopes his children will talk to their father about the trial rather than listening to gossip.

Chapter 10

- Atticus gives the children airguns.
- Rabid dog approaches.
- Atticus called home from work.
- A skilled marksman, Atticus kills the dog with a single shot.

The children regard Atticus as 'feeble' because he is 50 years old and never takes part in sports, such as shooting, as other, younger fathers do. By giving them airguns he allows them to shoot at birds, but insists the children 'remember it's a sin to kill a mockingbird', because mockingbirds do no harm — they simply sing. One Saturday the children spot a dog with rabies in the street. Calpurnia phones Atticus, who comes home immediately with Heck Tate, the sheriff, who asks Atticus to kill the dog because of Atticus's superior skill with a gun. Atticus reluctantly, but with great expertise, kills the dog instantly. Later his astonished children learn that their father gave up shooting long ago on moral grounds.

Chapter 11

- Mrs Dubose taunts the children.
- Jem vandalises her garden.
- Atticus makes Jem visit Mrs Dubose daily as a punishment.
- Death of Mrs Dubose, a former morphine addict.

Jem and Scout regularly pass the property of Mrs Henry Lafayette Dubose, whose 'vicious' habit is to sit on her porch and make aggressive remarks. 'Your father's no better than the niggers and trash he works for!' she says and Jem's control snaps. He bursts into Mrs Dubose's front yard and breaks all the old lady's camellia bushes. Atticus makes Jem apologise to Mrs Dubose and clear up the mess as well as calling each day to read to her. Mrs Dubose, now bedridden, usually falls asleep soon after the children arrive. Later that spring, she dies. Atticus explains that, very courageously, Mrs Dubose had overcome her addiction to a pain-killing drug at the end of her life.

Grade *focus*

In the A*–C grade range the examiners will expect to see not only that you know what happens in *To Kill a Mockingbird* but also that you recognise that it has a very distinct structure and shape. Use the following table to give yourself a clearer idea of what makes the difference between types of response in the higher and foundation tiers.

Grades A*–C	Grades D–G
Harper Lee uses a first-person child narrator whose story of two and a half years in Maycomb unfolds with wry comment from the 'hidden' adult Scout	Scout tells the story of two and half years of her childhood in Maycomb
Devices Lee uses to help the reader to see 'past' Scout include having her overhear conversations, and what others tell her — being told by other characters such as Jem, Miss Maudie and Dill about events at which she has not been present and discussions with Atticus and her own adult hindsight	Scout describes what happened to her
Part One leads to the trial, sets the scene and shows the children learning. Part Two is devoted to the trial and its aftermath with the incident with Bob Ewell and the final meeting with Boo Radley emerging from the central event of Part Two like a coda (or tailpiece) in music. Effectively the novel has two climaxes, the second of which leads to a very quiet conclusion as Scout falls asleep	The novel is in two halves

Pause for thought

A subheading for Part One of *To Kill a Mockingbird* could be 'Lessons the children learn'. Think carefully and list everything you can think of that Scout, Jem and Dill learn during the first 11 chapters, ranging from small, apparently trivial things to major lessons in life. It may be a good idea to organise your ideas in a table with three columns, one for each child.

Part Two

Chapter 12

- Jem is growing up and becoming distant.
- Children go to Calpurnia's 'black' church.
- Collection for Tom Robinson's family.
- Aunt Alexandra unexpectedly moves in.

Now 12, Jem is moody and less inclined to spend time with Scout. Calpurnia tries to comfort her but tells her this is inevitable. When, in Atticus's absence, Calpurnia is in charge of the children, she takes them to her church. There Lula tells Calpurnia she should not bring white children,

but everyone else makes Scout and Jem welcome. Few blacks can read hymn books. Reverend Sykes coaxes a generous sum for Helen Robinson out of the poor congregation. Back home Aunt Alexandra is waiting for the Finch children.

Chapter 13

- Aunt Alexandra entertains Maycomb's ladies.
- Aunt Alexandra's belief in family 'streaks'.
- Finch family history and Maycomb's social class or 'caste system'.
- Atticus's attitude to unquestioning family pride.

Aunt Alexandra, who has strong beliefs and prejudices, thinks the children are not being brought up properly. She believes that each Maycomb family has its own definite inherited tendencies. Atticus has agreed that she should stay but his views differ from his sister's. When she wants him to educate his children in family history and the 'gentle breeding' that makes the Finches 'fine folks', Atticus makes fun of it. Mildly resentful, the children accept Aunt Alexandra's arrival as an adult decision.

Chapter 14

- Gossip about the Finch family in town.
- Disagreements about Calpurnia.
- Runaway Dill found under Scout's bed.

The children are aware of growing hostility towards Atticus. In town Scout hears the word 'rape,' which she does not understand. A horrified Aunt Alexandra discovers that the children have been to Calpurnia's church and tells Atticus to get rid of her. Scout then overhears Atticus tell Aunt Alexandra that 'Calpurnia's not leaving this house until she wants to'. At bedtime Scout mistakes something beneath her bed for a snake but it turns out to be Dill in hiding. Atticus supplies food and contacts Dill's family.

Chapter 15

- Dill to stay in Maycomb for a week.
- Tom Robinson's sympathisers warn Atticus.
- Jem, Scout and Dill creep to Maycomb jail after dark.
- Atticus 'guards' Tom Robinson.
- Lynch party from Old Sarum wants Tom.
- The situation is defused when Scout innocently speaks to Mr Cunningham.

Tactful intervention by Atticus gets Dill a week in Maycomb. The trial is imminent. Tom Robinson is now in Maycomb jail and trouble is likely so Atticus calmly goes to the jail to keep watch. Without permission, the three children follow him after dark. Men arrive from Old Sarum to take and lynch Tom. The situation is dangerous, especially for the children, whom Atticus tries to send home. Eventually, Scout speaks politely, naturally and normally to Mr Cunningham, one of the lynching party, the innocence of which seems to remind Mr Cunningham of ordinary human behaviour. The men disperse.

Chapter 16

- Breakfast discussion of incidents at the jail.
- Trial attracts big numbers.
- Dolphus Raymond's 'mixed' family outside courthouse.
- Children sit with Reverend Sykes in black people's gallery in full courtroom.

Atticus talks about mobs, individuals and Mr Underwood's concern for black justice. Aunt Alexandra reprimands him for speaking in front of Calpurnia — a black servant to her but part of the family for Atticus (and Scout and Jem). People flock to the trial opening in holiday mood. Outside the courthouse the children see Mr Dolphus Raymond, who has a reputation as a heavy drinker. Married to a black woman, he has a family of 'mixed' children. The children get into the full courtroom only because Reverend Sykes invites them to sit in the 'coloured balcony'.

> **Key quotation**
>
> **'around here once you have a drop of Negro blood, that makes you all black'**
>
> (Jem, Chapter 16)

Chapter 17

- The first part of the trial.
- Heck Tate testifies to finding Mayella Ewell beaten up.
- Atticus establishes that no doctor was called to Mayella Ewell, that her right eye was injured and that Bob Ewell is left-handed.

Heck Tate explains that Bob Ewell sent for him. Mayella was lying hurt on the floor. She told the sheriff that Tom Robinson had injured and raped her, although there is no medical evidence. Atticus makes it clear that Mayella's right eye was hurt, not the left. This matters because a blow from a right-handed man, aimed straight, would normally land on the left of his victim's body. By asking Ewell to sign his name in court, Atticus demonstrates Ewell's left-handedness. It is therefore more likely that Ewell injured his daughter himself than that she was attacked by a right-handed person.

Chapter 18

- Mayella Ewell alleges Tom Robinson attacked her.
- Atticus's questioning shows Mayella's poverty, loneliness and deprivation.
- Hints in court that Bob Ewell beats his daughter.
- Tom Robinson's disabled left arm.

Mayella says she asked Tom Robinson, a black man she knows, onto her premises to chop wood. Then, she says, he attacked and 'took advantage' of her. Mayella is the eldest of seven motherless children who live in filth and poverty and for whom Mayella is expected to be responsible. She is 19, isolated and unhappy. Mayella almost admits her father's drunken violence but then draws back. Tom Robinson is asked to stand up. A childhood injury in a cotton gin (a machine used to process picked cotton) has made his left arm useless, so he could not have struck Mayella's right eye. And could a one-armed man have overpowered a 'strong girl' like Mayella, who claims he pinned her to the ground?

Chapter 19

- Tom Robinson's evidence.
- Tom's honesty and truthfulness.
- Tom testifies that Mayella 'hugged' and 'kissed' him.
- Tom admits sympathy for Mayella.
- Dill is upset.

Tom Robinson, aged 25, is shown to be an honest man. Atticus asks him about a previous conviction for fighting which he admits immediately. Tom's evidence is that, on the day in question, instead of leaving him to do the job in the yard, Mayella brought him into the house on a pretence, having sent the Ewell children into town. She then made sexual advances towards him. Tom tried to get away, but at that moment Bob Ewell looked through the window and was furious with his daughter. Tom ran away. Cross-questioned in court Tom says 'I felt right sorry for her', which prejudices almost all the white listeners in court against him. Dill is moved to tears by events in court.

Chapter 20

- Dolphus Raymond is not an alcoholic.
- Atticus sums up his case.
- Atticus argues Tom's entitlement to the same justice as a white man.
- Calpurnia arrives.

Text **focus**

Look carefully at Chapter 19 from, '"Answer the question," said Judge Taylor' to 'Atticus sat down'. Read it several times.

- Tom Robinson speaks in a non-standard English dialect and a broad Southern American accent. To an extent, most of the characters in *To Kill a Mockingbird* do this because, even among educated people, the speech patterns of Alabama and Mississippi are distinctive. This use of **dialect** and **accent** ensures that readers never forget the setting of the action — Lee's novel is firmly rooted in its place and time. Lee's black speakers, however, generally have stronger accents and make more use of dialect than white ones. She uses **phonetic** (as it sounds) spellings such as 'suh' for 'sir', 'chillun' for 'children' and 'thout bein' for 'without being'.

- When Tom Robinson says 'She hugged me round the waist', he is, by Maycomb standards in the 1930s, alleging something very serious indeed. He is telling the court that he, a black man, was the subject of sexual advances from a white woman. Lee does not tell the reader in so many words that this allegation caused noise and exclamations from the people present — she leaves it to the reader's imagination. It is implied. All she says is that Judge Taylor uses his gavel and that order is restored. This is a good example of an author drawing the reader in so tightly that she or he does not need to be told certain things. It is highly skilled writing.

- Courtrooms are a bit like theatres and much of what goes on in them is essentially theatrical. Conversations are conducted in front of an audience and sometimes unexpected things happen. Look at the way Lee makes the dialogue run quickly and dramatically as it would in a play. Words fly backwards and forwards like a tennis volley.

- Look at the language Scout uses to describe Tom Robinson's appearance and behaviour in court, such as 'The witness swallowed hard'. Work out what these sentences tell you about Tom Robinson's state of mind. Why does Lee make Scout state these things in such a simple way?

- 'Tom Robinson's manners were as good as Atticus's.' What do you think Scout means by this? The evidence is in the few lines before this statement.

- Decide how effective you find Lee's use of dialect and accent in this scene. How else might she have achieved a similar effect?

Outside the court, Scout and Dill talk to Dolphus Raymond. The drink he offers them turns out to be Coca-Cola, not whisky. Back inside the court, Atticus is summing up and asking the jury to return a verdict of not guilty. He feels sorry for Mayella, whose circumstances are so pitiable through no fault of her own, but stresses that Tom's life matters more. Calpurnia walks into court with a note for Atticus. She is searching for the children.

Chapter 21

- Calpurnia takes the children home for supper.
- Atticus agrees they can return for the verdict.
- After a long time the jury finds Tom Robinson guilty.
- Black people in the court stand in respect as Atticus passes by.

Aunt Alexandra has sent Calpurnia to fetch the missing children but, once he realised they have heard the rest of the trial, Atticus says they can return later. The jury deliberates for a long time and is still out when the children get back. Eventually, the 12 men return a unanimous verdict that Tom Robinson is guilty. Jem is distressed because he had been confident that his father would win the case — although Atticus had known all along that he would not. As Atticus, exhausted, leaves the court alone, everyone in the black people's gallery stands up in silent respect.

Pause for thought

The concept of trial by jury is nearly eight centuries old. It dates back to the Magna Carta of 1215. The Magna Carta was a document that set out an agreement between King John of England and the people, saying that the power of the king would be reduced and that a parliament would be established. The original document is on display at the British Library in London. When the early settlers arrived in America from England in the sixteenth and seventeenth centuries, they took the principle of trial by jury with them. Having now read Harper Lee's story of Tom Robinson's trial, based on real 1920s and 1930s cases, how fair do you think it was? Would a trial in twenty-first century Britain be fairer? If so, why? Attitudes to trial by jury are beginning to change in Britain. Find out more about proposed changes and work out what you think about them.

Chapter 22

- Jem and Aunt Alexandra are both distressed by the verdict.
- Atticus plans an appeal.
- Grateful black people send gifts to Atticus.
- Bob Ewell spits at Atticus and swears revenge.

Jem weeps in distress. Aunt Alexandra also feels justice has not been done and she sympathises with Atticus. The next morning, Atticus is more positive and talks about an appeal against the verdict. Meanwhile, large piles of food are quietly delivered to the house. These are gifts from black people who want to thank Atticus for his willingness to stand up in public for equal rights and justice. Miss Stephanie Crawford and Miss Rachel Haverford report that Bob Ewell spat in Atticus's face in the post office before witnesses and promised to 'get him'.

Chapter 23

- Atticus relaxed about Bob Ewell's threat.
- Atticus talks about the law and evidence.
- Aunt Alexandra condemns the Cunninghams as 'trash'.
- Jem realises that Boo Radley chooses not to leave his house.

Atticus tells the children they have nothing to fear from Bob Ewell but Aunt Alexandra disagrees. Atticus discusses rape law and the bringing of evidence at some length with Jem and Scout. Scout wants to invite Walter Cunningham to the house again and is firmly told by Aunt Alexandra that she may not because the Cunninghams may be good folks, 'But they're not our kind of folks'. Jem tells her that he thinks Boo Radley stays indoors simply because he wants to.

Chapter 24

- The Missionary Society meets at the Finches' house.
- Scout wears a dress and Calpurnia serves cakes.
- The ladies help black people in Africa but are not aware of the poor blacks in Maycomb.
- Atticus and Calpurnia inform Helen Robinson of Tom's death.

Scout, the tomboy, is forced into a dress and made to attend a meeting of the Missionary Society. The hypocritical women at the meeting want to help the people of the Mruna tribe in Africa but are insensitively critical of the black people they see every day. Then Atticus arrives and interrupts the meeting. Tom Robinson has been shot dead while trying to escape from prison. Atticus asks Calpurnia to help him break the news to Tom's widow, Helen.

Chapter 25

- Jem tells Scout to put a harmless insect outside rather than kill it.
- Dill describes the scene when Helen Robinson learns of Tom's death.
- Mr Underwood reports the death in the *Maycomb Tribune*.

Jem insists that Scout take the 'roly-poly' under her bed outside and release it safely because 'they don't bother you'. Jem and Dill accompany Atticus and Calpurnia to the Robinson house and Scout recounts the story as it has been told to her by Dill. Interest in Tom's death is short-lived in Maycomb, but there is a forceful editorial by Mr Underwood in that week's *Maycomb Tribune*.

Chapter 26

- School starts in autumn 1935.
- Children pass Radley house daily and Scout remembers games of two years before.
- Miss Gates teaches Scout's class about Adolf Hitler and democracy.
- Jem is unaccountably irritable.

Dill is now at Mississippi for the new school term. Scout and Jem pass the Radley house on the way to school each day. At school, a current events lesson leads to a discussion about Adolf Hitler's treatment of Jews in Germany. At home, Scout tries to discuss these matters with Jem but he shouts her down because he does not want to think about it. Atticus tries to explain Jem's mixed feelings.

Chapter 27

- Bob Ewell is sacked for laziness from a government job.
- Ewell attempts to break into Judge Taylor's house.
- Ewell harasses Helen Robinson until stopped by Link Deas.
- Maycomb plans Halloween pageant.
- Scout to play the part of a piece of pork.

Bob Ewell gets a job through a government work creation scheme but loses it almost immediately. Someone — Ewell — tries to break into Judge Taylor's house one Sunday evening while the judge is reading. Link Deas has sympathetically found a job for Helen Robinson and has to stop her being threatened on the way to work by Bob Ewell. Aunt Alexandra sees all these developments as ominous. Meanwhile, the adults in Maycomb are planning a large-scale pageant for Halloween at the end of October. The focus of the pageant is local farmers' produce, so Scout is chosen for the unglamorous role of a piece of meat.

Chapter 28

- Scout and Jem chat about their old childish games.
- At the pageant, Scout falls asleep, misses a cue and feels silly.
- Scout and Jem walk home alone with Scout still in her costume. They are followed and attacked.
- Someone carries Jem, injured and unconscious, into the house.
- Heck Tate tells them that Bob Ewell is dead.

On their way to the pageant, Scout and Jem chat. At school, Scout misses her cue and looks silly (Jem is in the audience) so she does not want to see anyone. She and Jem wait until the crowd has dispersed before setting off for home on a quiet path through the trees. Scout keeps her costume on. She hears a voice, then rustling, breathing and footsteps. Suddenly the children are attacked by an unidentified assailant. Jem is injured but Scout is protected by the chicken-wire costume. A man picks up the unconscious Jem and carries him the last few yards home with Scout following. Atticus and Aunt Alexandra telephone for Dr Reynolds and Heck Tate.

An unknown man stands quietly in the corner of Jem's bedroom when Heck Tate informs them that Bob Ewell has been stabbed and is lying dead beneath a tree.

Chapter 29

- Aunt Alexandra is distressed.
- Scout tells Heck Tate about the attack.
- Scout's costume has saved her life.
- Scout realises their unknown rescuer is Boo Radley.

Everyone remains in Jem's bedroom except Aunt Alexandra, who goes to her own room. Scout tells Heck Tate as much as she can about the attack. Atticus explains about Scout's badly crushed costume, which Heck Tate believes saved her life. Suddenly, Scout looks at the pale, thin, silent man in the corner. 'Hey, Boo,' she says to him.

Chapter 30

- Scout surprised that the others know Boo.
- Atticus is courteous to Boo.
- Atticus thinks Jem killed Ewell and that the truth must be told.
- Heck makes Atticus understand that Boo killed Ewell.
- Heck insists that Boo will be protected by a lie.

Atticus gently corrects Scout who must address the visitor as Mr Arthur. Scout then realises that her father, Dr Reynolds and Heck all know Boo, whom Atticus treats with his usual courtesy and gentleness. Scout is surprised that, for the adults, Boo has never been a mystery figure. Atticus is convinced that Jem killed Ewell in self-defence and that all the normal processes of the law must be observed without a cover-up. Heck disagrees. Eventually, he gets Atticus to see it was Boo who killed Ewell and Boo who must be protected. They will say that Ewell fell on his knife and killed himself. Atticus is eventually persuaded, although he remains troubled.

Chapter 31

- Scout takes Boo to say goodnight to Jem.
- Scout walks home with Boo.
- Standing on the Radley porch, she sees the street from Boo's point of view.
- Back home, she falls asleep while Atticus is reading to her.
- Atticus puts Scout to bed.

Boo is led by Scout to Jem's bedroom to bid the sedated boy goodnight. Childlike, he then asks Scout to take him home. Scout returns home where Atticus is sitting at Jem's bedside quietly reading a book of Jem's to himself. Scout asks him to read *The Grey Ghost* aloud to her. She soon falls asleep. When Atticus is putting her to bed, Scout tells him she has heard the whole story — about a misunderstood boy who turned out to be 'real nice'.

Pause for thought

Is it ever right to tell a lie? Atticus's whole professional and personal life has been built on telling the truth. Is he right to depart from that now? Scout tells us that he 'sat looking at the floor for a long time'. Then he says to his daughter, 'Mr Ewell fell on his knife. Can you possibly understand?' (Chapter 30) Does she? Does the reader?

Timeline

Year	Time of year	Chapter	What happens
		Part One	
1933	Early summer	1	The main characters are introduced. Scout is six
	September	2	Dill leaves Maycomb. Scout starts school. Description of the Cunninghams
	September	3	Description of the Ewells
1934	Spring/early summer	4	The children are intrigued by Boo Radley, who leaves gifts in a tree. Dill returns to Maycomb
	Spring/early summer	5	The children try to entice Boo outside by delivering a letter
	Late summer	6	The children creep up to the Radleys' house
	October/ November	7	Boo leaves more gifts in the tree before Nathan blocks the hole
	Winter	8	Snowfall in Maycomb. Miss Maudie's fire
	Christmas	9	Atticus agrees to defend Tom Robinson. Christmas at Aunt Alexandra's
1935	February	10	Atticus shoots a rabid dog
	Spring	11	Jem destroys Mrs Dubose's camellias and has to read to her. Mrs Dubose dies
		Part Two	
1935	Summer	12	The children are taken to First Purchase Church by Calpurnia. Aunt Alexandra arrives
	Summer	13	Aunt Alexandra entertains Maycomb's ladies
	Summer	14	Dill returns to Maycomb
	Summer	15	The lynch mob from Old Sarum tries to take Tom from jail. Scout talks to Mr Cunningham

Year	Time of year	Chapter	What happens
1935	Summer	16	The trial starts. The children sit in the black people's gallery
	Summer	17	Heck Tate and Bob Ewell testify
	Summer	18	Mayella Ewell testifies
	Summer	19	Tom Robinson gives evidence
	Summer	20	Scout and Dill learn the truth about Dolphus Raymond
	Summer	21	The jury finds Tom Robinson guilty
	Summer	22	Jem is upset by the verdict. The black community sends gifts to Atticus. Bob Ewell spits at Atticus and vows revenge
	Summer	23	Atticus is relaxed about Bob Ewell's threat
1935	August	24	Tom tries to escape from jail and is shot dead
	September	25	Dill describes how Helen Robinson is told of Tom's death
	September	26	School starts. Miss Gates teaches about Hitler and the Jews
	October	27	Bob Ewell attempts revenge on Judge Taylor and Helen Robinson. A pageant is planned
	October	28	Scout prepares for the pageant. Scout and Jem are attacked by Bob Ewell. Boo saves them by stabbing Ewell
	October	29	Boo is revealed as the children's saviour
	October	30	Atticus thinks Jem has killed Bob Ewell. Heck Tate proves it was Boo
	October	31	Boo and Scout visit Jem. Scout takes Boo home

Structure

Harper Lee divided *To Kill a Mockingbird* into two parts; Chapters 1–11 form the first part and Chapters 12–31 the second part.

Part One ends with the death of Mrs Dubose and Jem's reaction to it. Jem is still a young boy who 'buried his face in Atticus's shirt front'.

The opening of Part Two finds Jem, now 12, 'difficult to live with, inconsistent, moody'. Scout is puzzled that 'This change in Jem had come about in a matter of weeks' and Calpurnia wisely tells her 'I just can't help it if Mister Jem's growin' up…so you come right on in the kitchen when you feel lonesome. We'll find lots of things to do in here'. By changing the atmosphere between Scout and Jem, Harper Lee is moving the novel into another, more adult, mood for Part Two.

Part One shows the three children — Scout, Jem and Dill — learning lessons about life and people. Part Two deals with the lead-up to the trial, the trial itself and its aftermath.

Harper Lee could potentially have divided her novel into three sections, with two sections being made out of Part Two. There is a natural break at the end of Chapter 21 when the trial ends. This is also one of the most dramatic and moving moments in the novel as the jury members say 'Guilty…guilty…guilty' and Scout notices Jem, whose 'hands were white from gripping the balcony rail, and his shoulders jerked as if each "guilty" was a separate stab between them'. The chapter ends with all the black people in the gallery rising to their feet in a powerful gesture of silent respect because, as Reverend Sykes tells Scout, 'Your father's passin'.

Pause for thought

What exactly do the children learn in Part One? Make a detailed list. The obvious starting points are what they learn from their encounters with Boo Radley, Mrs Dubose and Walter Cunningham and what Atticus teaches them, but there are several others. If you include page and chapter references, this will form a useful part of your revision notes.

The central section of *To Kill a Mockingbird* takes place over a short period of time. Harper Lee makes it more exciting by quickening the pace. Everything that happens occurs within a few weeks during the summer of 1935. This is in contrast to Part One, the main events of which are spread over nearly two years.

After the trial, the action slows again with the last events of the novel spread over about three months. However, remember that although the trial of Tom Robinson is the central climax of the novel, 'our longest journey together', in which Jem is seriously injured by Bob Ewell, comes in Chapter 28. This episode forms another climax and one that directly affects the children and Atticus.

This is an unusual structure because in most novels the main climax comes near the end. Here it is as if the second, or subsidiary, climax has bounced off the first. Bob Ewell is trying to get his revenge for what he regards as Atticus's betrayal in court. The irony is that justice was not done in the court of law, but Lee wants the reader to agree that moral justice is done in the woods in Chapter 28.

Harper Lee is skilled in maintaining her reader's interest. Notice, for example, how she brings the children out of the court in Chapter 20 for their talk with Dolphus Raymond. As you read it, you wonder what is happening inside the courtroom. It is a way of heightening the suspense.

Something similar happens in Chapter 21 when the jury is 'out' coming to its conclusion and Calpurnia insists on taking the children home for supper. We are left, like Scout, desperate to get back to the court.

Look at the introduction of Boo Radley as a flesh-and-blood human being in Chapter 29. This is the first, and only, time we 'meet' him. Before this he is a shadowy figure who leaves little gifts (Chapters 4 and 7), repairs torn trousers (Chapter 7), or who puts a protective blanket round a child's shoulders (Chapter 8). Scout mistakes him for 'some countryman I did not know' and, for a while, the reader is taken in too. It is not until the end of Chapter 29, where Lee allows Scout three full and detailed paragraphs to describe the pale and troubled Boo, that we realise who Jem's rescuer is. Lee springs this surprise with great skill.

Review your learning

1 Who says 'Arthur Radley just stays in the house, that's all'?

2 What is the name of:

   a Aunt Alexandra's husband?

   b their grandson?

3 Who gives Helen Robinson a job after Tom's death?

4 What does Reverend Sykes make his people do at the end of Chapter 21? Explain why.

5 *To Kill a Mockingbird* is told in 31 chapters. Where are the main events and turning points?

6 What do you regard as the climax of *To Kill a Mockingbird*?

 More interactive questions and answers online.

Characterisation

- **Who are the characters?**
- **What are they like?**
- **How does Harper Lee present them?**
- **How do the characters relate to each other?**
- **What part do they play in the plot?**
- **How do they fit into the novel's themes and ideas?**

Jean Louise ('Scout') Finch

Scout says

- 'Atticus, are we going to win it [the court case]?' (Chapter 9)
- 'Don't you remember me, Mr Cunningham? I'm Jean Louise Finch.' (Chapter 15)
- 'I think there's just one kind of folks. Folks.' (Chapter 23)
- 'Hey, Boo.' (Chapter 29)

Scout

- narrates the story
- can read, so is frustrated by school
- fights against injustice with her fists until she learns self-control
- is curious — although increasingly sympathetic — about Boo Radley
- likes to play with her elder brother and not to be left out
- resents her Aunt Alexandra and sometimes Calpurnia
- admires, loves and respects her father
- visits Calpurnia's church
- attends the trial of Tom Robinson
- takes part in a pageant at school
- is there when Jem is injured by Bob Ewell, who is then killed by Boo Radley

Scout thinks that

- every human being should be taken at face value irrespective of skin colour or social class
- Atticus is an almost infallible source of wisdom and guidance
- Jem, Calpurnia and Miss Maudie all know things that she does not
- Tom Robinson is the victim of terrible injustice

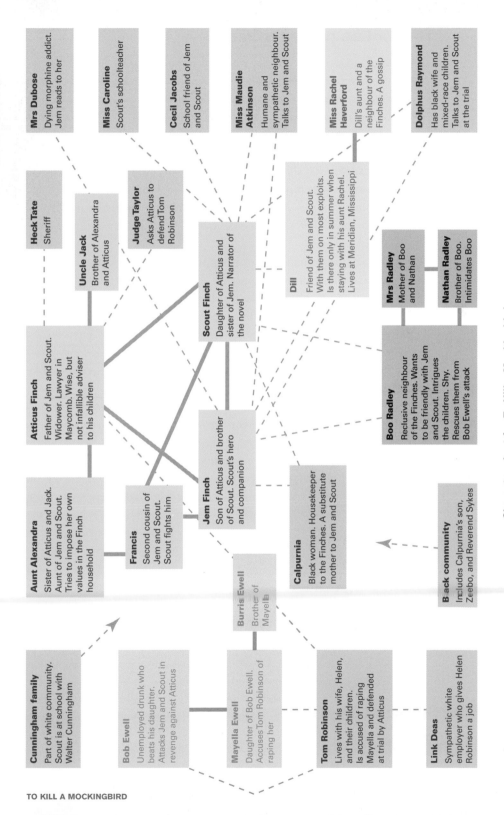

Mrs Dubose
Dying morphine addict. Jem reads to her

Miss Caroline
Scout's schoolteacher

Cecil Jacobs
School friend of Jem and Scout

Miss Maudie Atkinson
Humane and sympathetic neighbour. Talks to Jem and Scout

Miss Rachel Haverford
Dill's aunt and a neighbour of the Finches. A gossip

Dolphus Raymond
Has black wife and mixed-race children. Talks to Jem and Scout at the trial

Heck Tate
Sheriff

Uncle Jack
Brother of Alexandra and Atticus

Judge Taylor
Asks Atticus to defend Tom Robinson

Scout Finch
Daughter of Atticus and sister of Jem. Narrator of the novel

Dill
Friend of Jem and Scout. With them on most exploits. Is there only in summer when staying with his aunt Rachel. Lives at Meridian, Mississippi

Mrs Radley
Mother of Boo and Nathan

Nathan Radley
Brother of Boo. Intimidates Boo

Atticus Finch
Father of Jem and Scout. Widower. Lawyer in Maycomb. Wise, but not infallible adviser to his children

Boo Radley
Reclusive neighbour of the Finches. Wants to be friendly with Jem and Scout. Intrigues the children. Shy. Rescues them from Bob Ewell's attack

Aunt Alexandra
Sister of Atticus and Jack. Aunt of Jem and Scout. Tries to impose her own values in the Finch household

Jem Finch
Son of Atticus and brother of Scout. Scout's hero and companion

Francis
Second cousin of Jem and Scout. Scout fights him

Calpurnia
Black woman. Housekeeper to the Finches. A substitute mother to Jem and Scout

Cunningham family
Part of white community. Scout is at school with Walter Cunningham

Black community
Includes Calpurnia's son, Zeebo, and Reverend Sykes

Bob Ewell
Unemployed drunk who beats his daughter. Attacks Jem and Scout in revenge against Atticus

Burris Ewell
Brother of Mayella

Mayella Ewell
Daughter of Bob Ewell. Accuses Tom Robinson of raping her

Tom Robinson
Lives with his wife, Helen, and their children. Is accused of raping Mayella and defended at trial by Atticus

Link Deas
Sympathetic white employer who gives Helen Robinson a job

Character chart for *To Kill a Mockingbird*
Unbroken lines indicate family relationships

Harper Lee presents Scout

- entirely through the character's own words
- by sometimes letting us see 'past' Scout to reveal how she is seen by other characters
- by showing us Scout in a variety of situations

Scout believes that Atticus is an almost infallible source of wisdom and guidance

Conclusions

Scout is sensitive (see the incident with Mr Cunningham at the jail in Chapter 15 and how gently she speaks to Boo Radley in Chapter 30). She is also intelligent. 'Scout yonder's been readin' ever since she was born,' Jem tells Dill in Chapter 1. Atticus habitually addresses her as if she were almost adult.

Scout's affectionate nature is obvious in the way she relates to Atticus and Calpurnia. She adores Jem who, as her older brother, has almost the status of a hero in her life. Notice too how attached she is to Dill: 'With him, life was routine, without him, life was unbearable,' she remarks in Chapter 12.

She is not 'ladylike' which causes tension when Aunt Alexandra first comes to stay. Scout is more comfortable with male companions like Atticus, Jem and Dill.

Universal/The Kobal Collection

As well as being thoughtful and perceptive, she is impulsive and has a fiery temper. See the fights with Walter Cunningham (Chapter 3) and Cecil Jacobs (Chapter 9). She also fights second cousin Francis (Chapter 9) and there is a fight with Jem in Chapter 14. Nevertheless she eventually follows Atticus's advice to fight with her head. At the end of the novel the more mature nine-year-old Scout is less likely to get involved in fist fighting.

Scout has no prejudices — unlike Bob Ewell, Nathan Radley, Miss Stephanie Crawford and the Cunninghams. She is a child, with a child's approach to life and a child's mind, so she sees things as they are. In Scout's opinion, Calpurnia, Tom Robinson and the rest of the black community are simply human beings and she makes no distinction.

Atticus Finch

Atticus says

- 'You never really understand a person until you consider things from his point of view…until you climb into his skin and walk around in it.' (Chapter 3)
- 'it's a sin to kill a mockingbird' (Chapter 10)
- 'before I can live with other folks I've got to live with myself. The one thing that doesn't abide by majority rule is a person's conscience' (Chapter 11)
- 'It's not okay to hate anybody.' (Chapter 26)

Atticus

- defends Tom Robinson on a charge of rape
- shoots a rabid dog
- talks patiently to his children
- is always courteous
- underestimates Bob Ewell
- is highly respected by most Maycomb people

Atticus thinks that

- humans can live peacefully together only if they empathise with each other
- tolerance is essential
- for a Christian the teaching of Christ underpins every attitude and action
- all races should be treated equally

Harper Lee presents Atticus

- through Scout's point of view so that we see intimate moments in family life
- in court
- relating to the residents of Maycomb, such as Miss Maudie, Heck Tate and Mr Underwood
- as treating Calpurnia with courtesy and respect
- as teaching his children how to behave by example

Conclusions

'Civilized in his heart' Atticus, who has the respect of decent citizens such as Miss Maudie, Heck Tate, Judge Taylor, Calpurnia and Reverend Sykes is asked by Judge Taylor to take on the Tom Robinson rape case. Although

Atticus knows his children will suffer taunts because of it, he believes he must take on the case — a matter of conscience and self-respect. 'If I didn't I couldn't hold up my head in town, I couldn't represent this county in the legislature, I couldn't even tell you or Jem not to do something again,' he tells Scout in Chapter 9.

Atticus stands for Christian values. He tries to practise forgiveness and tolerance. Look, for example, at the way he behaves to Mrs Dubose in Chapter 11. Harper Lee contrasts his attitude with the hypocritical Christians in the novel, such as the ladies at Aunt Alexandra's Missionary Society in Chapter 24.

Atticus is a conscientious father who always makes time to talk to his children. His parenting skills are contrasted in the novel with those of Mr Radley, Bob Ewell and — more distantly — Dill's parents. He also disciplines his children firmly when he thinks it is necessary. He stops them playing 'One Man's Family' in Chapter 4, for instance. However, Atticus also makes mistakes as a father. He underestimates the seriousness of Bob Ewell's threats after the trial and exposes his children to serious risk as a result.

He is presented as an embodiment of everything Harper Lee respects in a lawyer, citizen, Christian and father. He is the moral centre of *To Kill a Mockingbird*.

Gregory Peck as Atticus Finch

Jeremy ('Jem') Finch

Jem says

- [of Boo] 'Ain't scared, just respectful' (Chapter 1)
- [at Calpurnia's church] 'Let's go home, Cal, they don't want us here' (Chapter 12)
- 'around here once you have a drop of Negro blood, that makes you all black' (Chapter 16)
- 'don't fret, we've won it [the court case]…Don't see how any jury could convict on what we heard' (Chapter 21)
- 'If there's just one kind of folks, why can't they get along with each other? If they're all alike, why do they go out of their way to despise each other?' (Chapter 23)
- 'Run, Scout! Run! Run!' (Chapter 28)

Jem

- is intensely and childishly curious about Boo Radley at the beginning of the novel
- loses his temper and vandalises Mrs Dubose's camellias
- provides a commentary on the trial for Scout and the reader
- is injured in the attack by Bob Ewell
- is a silent (sleeping) presence in the final scenes of the novel
- is nearly always with Scout

Jem thinks that

- all races should have equal rights
- Boo Radley is a reclusive monster, until he eventually works out that Boo remains in the house simply because he wants to stay inside
- Mrs Dubose is a spiteful old woman, until, with Atticus's help, he learns to climb into her shoes and walk around in them
- Tom Robinson will get justice because of Atticus's fine advocacy, but he is wrong
- he and Scout will be safe walking home from the pageant but, again, he is wrong

Jem and Scout Finch
(Phillip Alford and Mary
Badham)

Universal/The Kobal Collection

Harper Lee presents Jem

- through Scout's point of view so that we see him as an older brother — sometimes wise, occasionally exasperating, often pretending to know more than he does, usually dependable
- as intelligent, perceptive and deeply interested in Atticus's work — it is not hard to foresee Jem's likely later profession
- in a range of situations, such as retrieving his trousers from the Radley house, reading aloud to Mrs Dubose and trying to protect Scout from serious danger after the pageant

Conclusions

Of all the characters in the novel, Jem is perhaps the one who changes most. At the beginning he is a young boy who spends hours playing childish games with Scout and Dill. By the end of the novel, he is a teenager lying unconscious and injured, having defended his sister from Bob Ewell and narrowly escaped with his life.

Jem learns an important lesson through his relationship with the malicious Mrs Dubose when he realises that there is more than one side to her. Although she is dying, she is bravely trying to overcome drug addiction. Atticus treats her with respect and courtesy which, as usual, provides a role model for Jem to copy.

By the beginning of Part Two Jem is 12 and growing away from Scout, who finds him 'difficult to live with, inconsistent, moody'. Jem understands the finer points of the trial and the workings of the law in a way that Scout does not. From time to time during the five trial chapters (17–21), he explains to her what is happening. As Jem grows up, the reader can see, through Scout, that he is becoming ever more like his father: '…they were somehow alike. Mutual defiance made them alike' (Chapter 15).

Charles Baker ('Dill') Harris

Dill

- stays in Maycomb with his aunt, Miss Rachel Haverford, each summer
- says of his family 'they do get on a lot better without me. I cannot help them any'
- lives in what Scout describes as 'a twilight world' of escapist make-believe
- joins in with the Boo Radley games at the beginning of the novel
- is with Scout and Jem when the Old Sarum lynching party confronts Atticus
- is with Scout and Jem at the trial

Pause for thought

In what ways do you think Jem and Atticus are alike? How does Harper Lee achieve this resemblance, considering their physical differences? How difficult do you think it is for a novelist to convey in writing family likenesses of manner and attitude?

Key quotation

'If there's just one kind of folks, why can't they get along with each other? If they're all alike, why do they go out of their way to despise each other?'

(Jem, Chapter 23)

● is used by Harper Lee to provide a contrasting, less stable, family background to the Finches

Conclusions

Presented as a sensitive child and almost another brother to Scout, Dill comes from Meridian in Mississippi and weaves fantasies to cover his own unhappiness. Scout misses him intensely when he returns home each autumn.

Dill is curious about Boo Radley even when Scout and Jem have grown out of the childish games. Harper Lee does not develop the character of Dill and does not allow him to grow up and change as Scout and Jem do.

In Chapter 14, Dill turns up unexpectedly in Scout's bedroom. 'They just wasn't interested in me,' he says of his parents, to Scout's amazement. This is just before the lynching party incident and the trial. So, Dill is with Scout and Jem when they creep out to the jail at night and again when they disobey the adults and attend the trial which he finds distressing.

Universal/The Kobal Collection

L–R: Jem (Phillip Alford) and Scout (Mary Badham) regard Dill (John Megna) as a third sibling

Arthur ('Boo') Radley

● says almost nothing
● never leaves the house during daylight
● is the victim of a bullying brother, Nathan, having previously been victimised by his parents
● is probably a gentle, timid, damaged man

- may have learning difficulties and suffer from depression
- is presented by Harper Lee as an almost invisible character
- tries to befriend the children in several ways
- saves Jem's, and probably Scout's, life when they are attacked by Bob Ewell

Boo Radley (Robert Duvall) is befriended by Scout at the end of the novel

Calpurnia ('Cal')

- is the black housekeeper to the Finch family and a mother figure to Scout and Jem
- comes to work daily and has a home of her own elsewhere, although neither Scout nor the reader sees it
- is older than Atticus (who is 50) and has a grown-up family including Zeebo, the refuse collector
- is literate
- has two speech styles: one for the black community and an 'educated' one for when she is with white people
- has firm ideas about behaviour and discipline
- is understanding and wise

- takes the children to First Purchase Church
- is presented by Harper Lee as a fully developed black character and an example of a sensible, respectable working black person with thoughts and feelings
- is the black person Scout knows best

Grade *focus*

When you are writing about the characters in *To Kill a Mockingbird*, the examiners will want to see not only that you know who the characters are and what they do but also that you understand their importance in the novel and to Harper Lee's purpose. Use this table to give yourself a clearer idea of the difference between a higher and a foundation tier answer to a question about Calpurnia.

Grades A*–C	Grades D–G
Mother figure (like Miss Maudie and Aunt Alexandra). Has raised a family of her own and understands children	Helps to bring up Scout and Jem
Values high standards of behaviour and manners	Strict with Scout but also kind
Is a link between black and white communities. Lee uses her to show the children and the reader everyday life in the black community	Understanding and protective
Has been with the Finch family all her life (Atticus regards her as part of it) and knows their history which is bound up with her own. Family attitude contrasted with Mrs Merriweather's 'sulky darky in the kitchen.'	Takes the children to her church
Has confidence and delegated responsibility in the household. Does not need permission to discipline the children. An example of a black person having equal status based on mutual respect	Devoted to the Finches

Bob Ewell

- falsely accuses Tom Robinson of raping his daughter, Mayella
- certainly beat Mayella and possibly raped her himself
- is a widower like Atticus
- has a large family ranging from the eldest, Mayella, who is 19, to much younger children including Burris
- lives on state benefits
- drinks and is violent
- is lazy
- continues to harass Helen Robinson after Tom's death
- attacks the children and breaks Jem's arm
- is killed by Boo Radley to save Jem and Scout

Key quotation

'She says she never kissed a grown man before an' she might as well kiss a nigger. She says what her papa do to her don't count.'

(Tom Robinson, Chapter 19)

Pause for thought

What makes Bob Ewell an unusual character in the novel compared with almost everyone else?

Universal/The Kobal Collection

Atticus (Gregory Peck) confronts Bob Ewell (James Anderson)

Tom Robinson

- is aged 25, married to Helen and a father of three children
- is well respected in his own black community
- has only one functioning arm following a cotton gin accident when he was 12
- is found guilty of attacking and raping Mayella Ewell
- tries to escape while in prison awaiting appeal
- is shot dead by prison guards

Atticus (Gregory Peck)
defends Tom Robinson
(Brock Peters) in court

Miss Maudie Atkinson

- is a neighbour of the Finches
- is humane, thoughtful and considerate like Atticus
- is liked by Scout and Jem
- talks to the children both about the Radleys and about the Robinson case
- is a keen gardener
- loses her home in a fire but takes it in her stride
- is critical of many of the other women in the town
- is an old friend of Atticus's brother, Uncle Jack

Other characters

Harper Lee mentions a large number of Maycomb people by name in *To Kill a Mockingbird*. They represent black and white, male and female, youth and age, different social classes and professions and a range of points of view. Together, they function like a chorus in a Greek drama or an opera. Sometimes they speak as individuals. Sometimes groups of them — like the Old Sarum lynching party (Chapter 15) or Aunt Alexandra's ladies (Chapter 24) — share an attitude. They include:

- Aunt Alexandra: Atticus's sister, who leaves her ineffectual husband and comes to live with the Finches (Chapter 12). Rather self-opinionated, she thinks Atticus is raising the children too open-mindedly and wants them to be reminded of the family's position in Maycomb's 'caste system'. Although she is appalled by the suggestion that Scout and Jem might be social visitors in Calpurnia's home (Chapter 14), she is sorry that Atticus loses the case (Chapter 22), is genuinely upset that Tom is dead (Chapter 24) and is horrified when Jem is attacked by Bob Ewell (Chapter 29). Harper Lee uses her to show us that the conflict and tensions in *To Kill a Mockingbird* are not clear-cut. Sometimes Aunt Alexandra is right — she realises how dangerous Bob Ewell is when Atticus does not.
- Heck Tate: the sheriff who asks Atticus to shoot the rabid dog (Chapter 10). He also gives evidence in court and insists at the end of the novel that he and Atticus will conceal the truth about Bob Ewell's death. He is presented as a decent man who respects Atticus.
- Judge Taylor: presides over the Tom Robinson case. Taylor wants the truth told and knows that only Atticus has the integrity to defend Tom properly. He is straight and fair in court, even though to Scout's eyes he seems not to be paying attention. Bob Ewell clearly resents him and attempts to burgle Judge and Mrs Taylor's home in the

autumn after the trial (Chapter 27). Judge Taylor is another example of a moderate man concerned for justice.

- Dolphus Raymond: a fairly prosperous white man with a black wife, whose 'mixed' children are sent to the North to avoid prejudice. He is reputed to be a drunk and an 'evil man', but Scout and Dill discover this is a lie. He feigns drunkenness to give people something to criticise him for. His function in the novel is to teach Scout and the reader not to accept things at face value.

- Link Deas: a white cotton farmer with a large number of black employees. Harper Lee uses him to show that employers can treat black workers decently (as Atticus does with Calpurnia but Mrs Merriweather does not with Sophy, Chapter 24). Link Deas employs Helen Robinson as a house servant after Tom's death and protects her from Bob Ewell's threats.

- Reverend Sykes: the black pastor at First Purchase Church. He makes the children feel welcome during their visit to the church with Calpurnia (Chapter 12). At the trial, he takes care of the children. Afterwards he makes his congregation, and the children, stand up in silent respect for Atticus (Chapter 21). Like Tom Robinson, he is an example of a respected and respectable man who just happens to be black.

- Mrs Henry Lafayette Dubose: a sick neighbour who criticises and goads Scout and Jem relentlessly, especially about Atticus's decision to defend Tom Robinson. Atticus punishes Jem for bad behaviour towards her by insisting that Jem go regularly to read to her (and Scout volunteers too). The old lady, whom the children find repugnant, is bedridden and clearly very ill. Later Atticus explains that Mrs Dubose has died in great pain because of determination to overcome her addiction to morphine, a painkiller. Like Dolphus Raymond, she teaches the children and the reader not to make assumptions about people.

- Other members of the Maycomb 'chorus' include Mr Underwood, the Cunninghams, Cecil Jacobs, Miss Rachel Haverford, Mr Avery, Miss Caroline Fisher, Chuck Little, Mayella Ewell, Burris Ewell, Helen Robinson and her children, Lula, Zeebo, Nathan Radley, Mr Horace Gilmer, Mrs Grace Merriweather and Mrs Gertrude Farrow.

Text focus

Look carefully at Chapter 19 from 'I know what you mean, boy' to 'all you gotta do is step back inside the courthouse' in Chapter 20. Read it several times.

- Scout has been told that Dolphus Raymond is an 'evil man' because he drinks. This is the first time she has met him face to face, so although she finds him 'fascinating', with his English riding boots and wholesome smell of 'leather, horses, cottonseed', she accepts his invitation to take a drink 'reluctantly'. Mr Raymond offers Scout and Dill a paper sack with straws in it. He knows what the children think and Scout comments that he was 'evidently taking delight in corrupting a child'. Actually, he is enjoying his own joke because, as Dill discovers when he takes a sip, the bag contains nothing but Coca-Cola.

- Harper Lee is revealing more of Dolphus Raymond's character through Scout's surprise and attitude. He says that he knows he will be criticised. 'Some folks don't — like the way I live' he tells the children, referring to his black wife and 'mixed' children whom the children know by sight. Scout describes him ironically as a 'sinful man who had mixed children and didn't care who knew it'. He argues that letting

people think he is a drunk gives people a reason to criticise him. Scout finds his reasoning odd and tells him that it is not honest to make 'yourself out badder'n you are already'. She comments with adult hindsight that he was deliberately perpetuating 'fraud against himself'. She fails to understand, as Atticus probably does, that he is deliberately deflecting criticism away from the people who matter to him — his wife and children.

- When Scout asks Mr Raymond why he has let them discover his 'deepest secret', he tells them it is because they are children and will understand, and he half-jokingly swears them to secrecy.

- The portrayal of Dolphus Raymond reminds the reader that all is not as it seems in Maycomb, where false assumptions are constantly made about people. It also reminds us that the town's racism is not total. Mr Raymond is humane and thoughtful in his eccentric way. His comment about 'the simple hell people give other people' cuts right to the heart of what *To Kill a Mockingbird* is about.

- In which ways is Atticus 'not a run-of-the-mill' man?

- Sum up what Scout learns from this encounter.

Review your learning

1 Who says 'If your father's anything, he's civilized in his heart'?

2 Name the character who says 'Will you take me home?'

3 Name three people who torment Scout and Jem about their father's intention to defend a 'nigger'.

4 How does Harper Lee make her characters interesting?

5 Which character in *To Kill a Mockingbird* is the most fully presented in your view?

 More interactive questions and answers online.

Themes

● **What are the novel's main themes?**
● **What do they add to the novel?**
● **How do themes work?**
● **What do you learn about Harper Lee's views from the themes she explores in *To Kill a Mockingbird* ?**

A theme is an idea, or a set of ideas, that is threaded through a piece of writing. Think of *To Kill a Mockingbird* as a piece of multi-coloured fabric. A theme is a single-coloured thread — red, blue, yellow and so on. Each thread is woven into the whole as part of the pattern. It mixes with the other colours that it crosses to make shapes or new colours. All the threads overlap. In the same way, Harper Lee weaves her ideas about family life, growing up or courage into the story that she is telling.

When we discuss a theme, it is as if we are pulling out a single thread from the novel's overall pattern. We can look at it on its own and then weave it back into the whole.

Remember these three points as you think about the themes in this novel:

1 No theme in a novel is completely separate from any other. They all overlap. That is what makes a text such as *To Kill a Mockingbird* feel complete, well constructed and satisfying.

2 Similar themes are often discussed using different names. For example, prejudice is close to intolerance, bigotry to hypocrisy, learning to education. Do not get too carried away in compiling long, repetitive lists of themes.

3 Some themes feature more regularly than others in the pattern of the novel.

Racism

To Kill a Mockingbird shows us the everyday racism of 1930s Alabama. Harper Lee makes sure we continually hear black people being derided and insulted as 'niggers', and the plot makes it clear that blacks are regarded as sub-human by the white community. For example, one of the reasons why Maycomb's whites so readily accept Tom Robinson's guilt is belief in the commonly held racial stereotype that black men had animalistic sexual urges and little self-control. Despite powerful evidence,

Tom is not thought worthy of a fair trial by many Maycomb inhabitants. That is why the lynching party, which includes Mr Cunningham, descends on the jail in Chapter 15. For the Robinson family, this racism is a form of hell, which leads to Tom's death at the hands of the white guards who casually shoot him when he panics and tries to scale the prison fence in a desperate escape attempt.

There are other instances of racism in the novel. Nathan Radley shoots at an imaginary black man when he thinks he is being burgled. Mrs Merriweather cruelly fails to understand what her servant Sophy is feeling.

The black characters have low expectations and low-paid jobs: a direct consequence of their segregated and poor-quality education. There are no blacks at Scout and Jem's school. Unusually, Calpurnia can read and write, but at her church very few members of the congregation are literate. Cal has taught her son Zeebo, who leads the hymn-singing, to read. Even so, there are no good jobs for black people. Zeebo is a refuse collector (he disposes of the rabid dog's corpse in Chapter 10) and he thinks he has done well. Although black people are used to this it adds up to a detailed picture of casual racism.

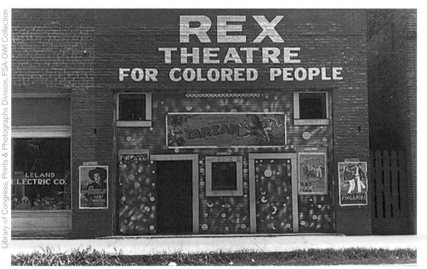

Library of Congress, Prints & Photographs Division, FSA-OWI Collection

During the 1930s, racial segregation was evident in all aspects of everyday life

Family

To Kill a Mockingbird presents us with many families, some happier and more successful than others. Some are more prominent. Others are mentioned only in passing. They include the Finches, Radleys, Ewells, Robinsons, Cunninghams, Dill's family and Calpurnia's family. Harper Lee wants us to think about different models of family life, to make comparisons and to draw our own conclusions.

However, because the story is told through Scout's narration, the Finch family is the only one that the reader can 'enter'. All the others are viewed from the outside. We are therefore led to compare other families with the Finches as Harper Lee develops this theme.

Atticus Finch is a widower and a single parent but his children are not disadvantaged or emotionally deprived. An intelligent, loving father, he provides his children with everything they need. Atticus talks to his children, teaches them things and listens to what they say. Notice how often Scout, who is only six when the novel opens, sits on her father's lap or close to him while they are talking. He also reads to her regularly. When Jem is injured at the end of the novel, Atticus will not leave his side. Harper Lee is presenting us with her ideal father.

Aunt Alexandra is part of the extended Finch family. We also meet her grandson Francis, with whom Scout quarrels (Chapter 9), and her non-descript husband, Uncle Jimmy. The third sibling is Uncle Jack, a doctor in the North, who returns to Finch's Landing each year for Christmas.

The Finch family is very close in the novel

Contrasting with the Finch family are the Ewells and the Radleys. Bob Ewell, like Atticus, is a widower. Instead of working, he prefers to live on state benefits and to spend most of his money on drink and he is violent. His large family of children are dirty, unmanageable (see the incident in Chapter 3 concerning Burris Ewell), incompetently cared for by Mayella and allowed to run wild.

Or take the Radleys. Boo is damaged and vulnerable — and is rumoured to have attacked his father years earlier with scissors — but no one in his family seems to treat him with the kindness and understanding he might have received if he had been born a Finch. When old Mrs Radley dies the community hardly notices. This is an unhappy family without children: neither brother is married so there is no real family life in the Finch sense.

Grade *focus*

Higher-tier candidates need to show not only that they know the events of the novel but also that they can think about its themes and ideas analytically. Use this table to work out the difference between a foundation and higher-tier answer to a question about family in *To Kill a Mockingbird*.

Grades A*–C	Grades D–G
Finch family an example of an ideal family — despite being motherless. Based on values Lee respects — truth, justice, education. Central to novel. Other families measured against — and compared with — it	Finch family loving and supportive
Robinsons shows reader that poverty is no barrier to high values. And that colour has nothing to do with family values	Robinson family black, poor and in trouble
Ewells in the novel to show that poor whites can be more culpable than poor blacks. Poverty and attitude are not colour-related. Bob Ewell is the central figure of evil in the novel. Mayella epitomises misfortune — worse off even than Helen Robinson, who has friends. At school Burris represents the everyday face of poverty and poor upbringing	Ewell family white, poor and in trouble
Radleys represent an unhappy misfortune very different from the Finches. Boo stands for everything which is vulnerable and misunderstood but harmless – like a mockingbird. Nathan, like a minor Bob Ewell, has no empathy and is cruel. They are the sons of misguided, inadequate parents — very different from Atticus	Radley family dysfunctional and troubled

Dill tells Scout in Chapter 14 that no one has any time for him at home. Given her own family experience, Scout simply cannot imagine or understand this.

The brief glimpse Harper Lee gives us of the Robinson family at home (Chapter 25) reminds us that family contentment and affection do not depend on being financially well off — or on skin colour.

The poor, but hard-working, Cunninghams — sometimes misguided but decent — are contrasted with other families too. One of the novel's most powerful moments is in Chapter 15 when Scout's innocent intervention suddenly makes Mr Cunningham remember family values.

Key quotation

I found myself wondering…what I would do if Atticus did not feel the necessity of my presence, help and advice. Why, he couldn't get along a day without me. Even Calpurnia couldn't get along unless I was there. They needed me.

(Scout, Chapter 14)

Mockingbirds

A member of the finch family, a mockingbird has dull grey feathers but it sings distinctively and often imitates (mocks) the calls of other birds.

In *To Kill a Mockingbird* it symbolises innocence and natural goodness. Like Tom Robinson and Boo Radley, mockingbirds are harmless and therefore should not be shot, killed or persecuted. When Atticus says 'Shoot all the bluejays you want, if you can hit 'em, but remember it's a sin to kill a mockingbird' he is quoting an old proverb.

Tom Robinson is like a mockingbird, partly because he is physically disabled. He is also socially 'disabled', his real weakness. He is a black man to whom a white woman has made sexual advances. Therefore, in the eyes of most people in Maycomb, he must be destroyed. Boo Radley's likeness to a mockingbird comes about because he is psychologically damaged. He is timid, childlike and almost incapable of being integrated into Maycomb society. He is an outsider and not properly understood, so he is seen as threatening. In this way, Harper Lee draws the elements of her mockingbird theme together by making us compare different characters and events in the novel.

She reinforces the point in Chapter 25 by making Mr Underwood, the newspaper proprietor and editor, write for his readers after the death of Tom Robinson that it 'was a sin to kill cripples, be they standing, sitting, or escaping'. Scout tells us that Mr Underwood 'likened Tom's death to the senseless slaughter of songbirds by hunters and children'.

> ### Key quotation
>
> 'Mockingbirds don't do one thing but make music for us to enjoy. They don't eat up people's gardens, don't nest in corncribs, they don't do one thing but sing their hearts out for us. That's why it's a sin to kill a mockingbird.'
>
> (Miss Maudie, Chapter 10)

> ### Pause for thought ⏸
>
> Some commentators on *To Kill a Mockingbird* say that Atticus is another 'mockingbird' because he 'sings his heart out' for Tom Robinson in court. How far do you agree with this?

Paul J. Fusco/SPL

A mockingbird — a symbol of innocence and natural goodness

At the end of the novel, Heck Tate tells Atticus that to bring Boo Radley to 'justice' would be a sin. 'It's a sin and I'm not about to have it on my head,' he says. Scout explains to Atticus that she understands this by saying: 'Well, it'd be sort of like shootin' a mockingbird, wouldn't it?'

Text **focus**

Look carefully at Chapter 31 from '"Will you take me home?"' to 'Just standing on the Radley porch was enough.' Read it several times.

- This passage relates to the novel's family theme because, as she stands on the Radley family porch, Scout reflects on the previous three years, seeing herself and Jem as 'Boo's children'. She also sees Boo for the first time as someone who belongs to the neighbourhood, which is an extension of the family. By presenting a rapid flashback using the third person ('he', 'they', 'the children', 'a man'), Scout sees events from a viewpoint outside her own and links together everything that has happened and all the themes in the novel, the climax of which is her ability to stand, with tolerance and understanding, in Boo's shoes — or at least on his porch.

- 'Boo's children needed him' is a simple, four-word statement. It is poignant because Boo is a cowed, timid individual, ill-treated by his family and misunderstood by most Maycomb inhabitants, such as Miss Stephanie Crawford. Note that Miss Stephanie is mentioned three times in this passage because her gossipy, judgemental character represents everything that makes Maycomb a 'tired old town' and contributes to its racism, intolerance and insularity which are threaded thematically through the novel. Yet, like everyone else, Boo thrives on being needed. He has long observed the children from a distance and wanted to be friends with them. When they are attacked in the wood by Bob Ewell, Boo can, at last, do something positive. He is a gentle, childlike person, which is why Harper Lee makes Scout use words like 'whispered', 'gently' and 'afraid'.

- What is there in this passage to remind you that Boo Radley is a 'mockingbird'?

- Which words and phrases show how much Scout has grown up in the three years covered by the novel?

- Who shows courage in this passage? Which words and phrases show this?

Courage

Various sorts of courage appear in *To Kill a Mockingbird*. Examples include Scout's insistence on going with Jem to Mrs Dubose's house (Chapter 11), Chuck Little's refusal to be intimidated by Burris Ewell (Chapter 3), Helen Robinson's stoicism when she is widowed (Chapter 27), Miss Maudie coping with the loss of her home (Chapter 8), Atticus waiting at the jail for the lynch mob (Chapter 15), Mrs Dubose overcoming her morphine addiction (Chapter 11), the children braving the Radley house (Chapter 4) and timid Boo Radley confronting Bob Ewell (Chapter 28).

In the Southern states in the 1930s, there was a long-established tradition of fierce, reckless 'shot-gun' courage essential to the character of the Southern 'gentleman'. For example Nathan Radley shoots at 'niggers'

when he thinks he is being burgled (Chapter 6) and men from Old Sarum think it is brave and right to go to the jail and demand that Tom Robinson be handed over to them (Chapter 15). Atticus, of course, lacks it. Hence Scout's rueful comment in Chapter 10: 'Atticus was feeble: he was nearly fifty.' 'He worked in an office, not in a drug-store. Atticus did not drive a dump-truck for the county, he was not the sheriff, he did not farm, work in a garage, or do anything that could possibly arouse the admiration of anyone,' comments the adult Scout looking back with irony, because, of course, Atticus was doing a great deal that was highly admirable. When Atticus shoots the rabid dog, Jem is delighted because, at last, he has discovered in his father a 'manly' skill that makes him more like other fathers.

Harper Lee wants Scout and Jem — and us — to understand that moral courage is far more important, and perhaps harder to achieve, than physical courage. After Mrs Dubose's death (Chapter 11) Atticus tells the children, 'I wanted you to see what real courage is, instead of getting the idea that courage is a man with a gun in his hand.'

Atticus's moral courage is Tom Robinson's only hope during his trial

Universal/The Kobal Collection

Atticus defends Tom Robinson because he courageously believes that he must. He knows he will fail, which makes his determination even braver. Atticus's moral courage is Tom's only hope at the trial. However, being true to his beliefs is difficult for Atticus. He is abused by towns-people such as Mrs Dubose (Chapter 11), Cecil Jacobs (Chapter 9) and his great-nephew Francis (Chapter 9). He knows that Scout and Jem have to bear this also. At the end of the novel, they are physically attacked by Bob Ewell because of their father's 'nigger-loving' beliefs and moral courage.

Growing up

During the novel's three years Harper Lee presents Scout and Jem (and, to a lesser extent, Dill) growing up and changing, partly because they are exposed to a series of planned and unplanned 'lessons'. You can take almost any chapter of *To Kill a Mockingbird* and find answers to the question: 'How does Harper Lee develop Scout's awareness and knowledge in this chapter?' (a likely GCSE passage-based question). As in real life, growing up is a continuous process.

Scout's learning mostly comes from Atticus who teaches her to control her impulsiveness (Chapter 9) and to recognise different sorts of courage (Chapters 10 and 11). He also tells her several times that tolerance and empathy ('another person's skin') are important and that sometimes you have to rise above other people's comments and attitude.

Scout is also taught manners by Calpurnia when Walter Cunningham comes to lunch (Chapter 3) and the value of being a 'lady' by Aunt Alexandra (Chapter 24). Uncle Jack teaches her something about adult perceptions of children (Chapter 9). From the teachers at school (Miss Caroline in Chapters 2 and 3, and Miss Gates in Chapter 26) she learns that many 'educated' adults are much less wise and more prejudiced and ignorant than Atticus.

Ironically, Scout believes she acquires little formal learning at school. She is more advanced than most of the other children and the teachers are not skilled in what would now be called mixed-ability teaching: 'I inched sluggishly along the treadmill of the Maycomb County school system' and 'I knew nothing except what I gathered from *Time* magazine and reading everything I could lay hands on at home' (Chapter 4).

Jem's increasing maturity is carefully charted through the novel too. Scout comments on the changes she notices, especially at the beginning of Part Two when Jem is 12. She is puzzled by the change in him, which 'had come about in a matter of weeks'. Calpurnia, herself the mother of at least

Key quotation

'You might hear some ugly talk about it at school, but do one thing for me if you will: you just hold your head high and keep those fists down. No matter what anybody says to you, don't you let 'em get your goat.'

(Atticus to Scout, Chapter 9)

one grown-up son, Zeebo, understands and tells Scout that Jem is 'gonna want to be off by himself a lot now, doin' whatever boys do'.

During the trial, it is the maturing Jem who explains to Scout what is going on and why, although he is deeply distressed by the outcome (Chapter 22).

Suffering caused by others

The 'simple hell' people impose on each other in *To Kill a Mockingbird* goes beyond the treatment of black people by whites. Mayella Ewell, for instance, lives with a brutal and drunken father. She has no money and no friends. Young as she is, she is expected to look after all the younger children. Part of Tom Robinson's 'crime' is that he, a happily married and decent family man, feels sorry for her — not something the prejudiced community approves of in a black man.

Dill is a deeply unhappy boy too. For all his fantasising, he is an unwanted child whose mother, far away in Mississippi, is too busy with her new husband to take any notice of him. Boo Radley suffers as well. He is a damaged and vulnerable human being, tyrannised first by his father and now by his brother.

Other themes

Lesser, but related, themes in the novel include:

- elimination of the dangerous for the benefit of the majority
- education
- hypocrisy
- tolerance
- justice

Review your learning

1 What do we mean by a theme?

2 List the most important themes in *To Kill a Mockingbird*.

3 Who are the main 'mockingbirds' in the novel?

4 What is the main sort of courage that interests Harper Lee?

5 What did Dolphus Raymond mean by 'the simple hell people give other people'?

6 Which character in *To Kill a Mockingbird* do you think grows up and changes the most?

 More interactive questions and answers online.

Style

- **How does the author tell her story?**
- **From whose points of view does the reader learn about events and characters?**
- **Where and when is the novel set and what effect does this have?**
- **How does Harper Lee create atmosphere?**
- **What use does she make of colourful description?**
- **What sort of language does she use and why?**

In the examination, style includes looking at **language, form and structure**, which are key elements of **Assessment Objective 2 (AO2)** (see page 71 for further details)

Viewpoint

The story is told entirely by Jean Louise ('Scout') Finch. As she is part of the events she is describing, Scout the narrator uses pronouns such as 'I', 'me', 'mine', 'we', 'us' and 'ours'. This technique is known as **first-person narrative**. Although first-person narratives are realistic, writing in this style presents the author with technical problems which would not exist if the story were told in the **third person**, i.e. by someone outside the story describing the activities, thoughts and views of the characters.

In a first-person narrative such as *To Kill a Mockingbird* the story is restricted to events witnessed by the narrator. Harper Lee gets round this fairly smoothly by using other characters to give Scout information. For example, when Scout tells the story of Simon Finch in Chapter 1, she is relying on what other people have told her. Most of her background information about the Radleys comes from Miss Maudie and Atticus. Dill tells Scout about the visit to the Robinson house in Chapter 25. Sometimes Scout overhears things such as the conversation between Atticus and Uncle Jack in Chapter 9 and between Atticus and Aunt Alexandra in Chapter 14.

Harper Lee does not restrict herself to one point of view. Other opinions are simply filtered through Scout, and the reader learns to allow for a child's exaggerations and distortions. When Atticus is telling Scout why she has to go to school in Chapter 3, although the Ewells do not, we can see 'past' Scout and understand Atticus's point of view. Another example is Lula's racist confrontation of the white children at First Purchase Church

in Chapter 12. We share Scout and Jem's uncomfortable feelings, but we can understand how Lula feels too.

Remember there are two Scouts in *To Kill a Mockingbird*: the young girl aged six to nine who lives in the early 1930s and the adult Scout looking back many years later. 'When enough years had gone by to enable us to look back on them, we sometimes discussed the events leading to his [Jem's] accident,' she says in the novel's second paragraph.

Although the child Scout is the main character in the story, the adult Scout narrates. Although we never 'meet' the adult Scout and know nothing directly about her after the age of nine, Harper Lee's use of this 'hidden' adult narrator means she can use adult language and express things from an adult point of view.

Text focus

Look carefully at the opening of Chapter 16, from the start to 'She knows what she means to this family'. Read it several times.

- Jem and Scout (with Dill) have disobediently left the house the previous evening and gone to the town jail where Atticus was protecting Tom Robinson with his presence. Aunt Alexandra radiates 'waves of disapproval' as she sips her breakfast coffee. She is cold in her manner and cross because 'children who slipped out at night were a disgrace to the family'. Calpurnia, on the other hand, is presented here as much warmer and more loving. She gives in to Scout's pleading, as a gesture of sympathy, and gives her a drop of coffee with plenty of comforting milk while Aunt Alexandra issues a 'warning frown'. She is put out because Atticus has been humorously commenting on Braxton Underwood's self-contradictory attitude to blacks, which Aunt Alexandra thinks is inappropriate in front of Calpurnia. The point here is that Atticus and the children regard Calpurnia as a member of the family. To Aunt Alexandra, she is just a servant — one of 'them' — before whom certain things should not be said. Perhaps, too, Aunt Alexandra is jealous of Calpurnia's status in the family. The children's aunt has moved in to be a substitute mother, but Calpurnia is already warmly fulfilling that role. These subtleties are embedded in the style.

- Scout is looking back and analysing what happened and what people felt from an adult perspective. As a child, she would not have used expressions like 'frank admiration', 'fey fit of humour' or 'outright irritation', yet her childishness is clearly presented through the use of expressions she would have used at the time such as 'awfully nice'.

- Jem is presented here as having been distressed the previous evening but feeling stronger this morning. That is why he can eat three eggs for breakfast. Atticus is not angry with his children for following him into town the night before. He teases his sister and annoys her: 'Atticus said he was right glad his disgraces had come along.' His mood turns though when Aunt Alexandra criticises his attitude to Calpurnia and a 'faint starchiness' comes into his voice as he declares that 'Anything fit to say at the table's fit to say in front of Calpurnia'.

- What do you learn here — through Scout from Atticus — about Braxton Underwood?

- Look at the balance Harper Lee uses in this passage between **direct speech** ('he asked') and **reported speech** ('children who slipped'). How well do you think this mixture works? Explain your views.

The young Scout would never have said 'After one altercation' (Chapter 12) or 'No economic fluctuations changed their status' (Chapter 17).

Setting and atmosphere

The novel is set almost entirely in Maycomb. Only once, and very briefly, does the action shift anywhere else — when Atticus takes the children a few miles out of town to spend Christmas with his sister's family at Finch's Landing (Chapter 9).

Other places are mentioned. Dill arrives each summer from Meridian in the neighbouring state of Mississippi, Atticus is often away working in Alabama's state capital Montgomery, Uncle Jack visits from the North and Tom Robinson is imprisoned and dies at a jail some distance from Maycomb. However, Scout and Jem stay in Maycomb — 'a tired old town'.

Many of the town's inhabitants have limited vision because they have no experience of any other location. Lee makes fun of this insularity when she presents us with the Maycomb Missionary Society ladies in Chapter 24. They think they care deeply about an impoverished tribe in remote Africa, but are hard and unfeeling about poor black residents in their own community.

The Maycomb setting is crucial to what happens in *To Kill a Mockingbird*. Tom Robinson's conviction would not have happened in the Northern states of America (where Dolphus Raymond sends his children to protect them from prejudice, and where Uncle Jack practises as a doctor). In the North, slavery was never part of everyday life and so large communities of poor, disadvantaged blacks did not develop as they did in the South after slaves were freed.

Remember that the novel is set in a particular time, as well as a particular location. The early 1930s was a time of great poverty for Southern farmers and their surrounding communities. The poverty and the relatively recent slavery meant that there was tension between the different racial groups. It is this atmosphere that Harper Lee depicts so effectively in *To Kill a Mockingbird*. As you study the novel, pay attention to the way in which Lee uses literary style to reflect the tension in events.

As soon as word gets out that Atticus will defend Tom Robinson, the comments start: 'we would squirm our way through sweating sidewalk crowds and sometimes hear "There's his chillun," or "Yonder's some Finches"' (Chapter 14). Although the young Scout does not understand the implications of some of this and, on one occasion, goes home to ask Atticus what rape is, she is well aware that animosity is building up. The tension is tightened through the aggressive remarks of Francis Finch, Cecil Jacobs and most particularly the 'vicious' Mrs Dubose (Chapter 11). Because Mrs

Dubose is an adult, it hurts more, and her comments inflame Jem so that he loses his temper and vandalises her garden.

The atmosphere in court is dramatic and tense because a number of people are 'performing' in public, including Atticus, Judge Taylor and all the people who give evidence. Yet no one can be sure of the outcome. Atticus tells Scout in Chapter 9 that there is no chance of his winning the case for Tom. Reverend Sykes tells the children, 'I ain't ever seen any jury decide in favour of a coloured man over a white man' (Chapter 21).

Harper Lee builds up suspense by running the trial through several chapters and taking the children out for breaks. There is a great sense of disappointment when the jury returns its guilty verdict in Chapter 21. Jem weeps bitterly. The temporarily exhausted Atticus shows signs of strain, too, for the first time: 'Seems that only children weep,' he comments bitterly in Chapter 22.

In the last third of the book, after the trial, Harper Lee builds up an atmosphere of suspense in anticipation of Bob Ewell's attack. She does this by having Scout mention seemingly trivial things like Ewell spitting at Atticus, losing his job and being suspected of an attempted break-in at Judge Taylor's house. Atticus sees no threat but Aunt Alexandra is convinced (rightly, as it turns out) that Ewell will attempt something 'furtive'. As the children leave for the pageant, Scout solemnly mentions setting out on 'our longest journey together' — a signal to the reader that something dramatic is coming (Chapter 27).

In the wood, on their return journey, a tense atmosphere of fear and danger is created and heightened by Scout's being encased in her pageant costume. She cannot see what is going on. The reader can only experience what she can remember feeling, hearing and smelling: 'the soft swish of cotton', 'I felt the sand go cold under my feet', 'His stomach was soft but his arms were like steel'.

The novel ends in an atmosphere of great peace and tranquillity. Jem is asleep, Bob Ewell is dead, Atticus is overwhelmed with relief, Aunt Alexandra is so overcome with (unfounded) guilt that she withdraws from the scene. Scout accompanies the pale, timid Boo Radley home in the moonlight. Atmospherically, this is a scene sharply contrasted with the skirmish with Ewell in the wood and the unjust hostility of the trial. Finally, Scout falls asleep in her own bed.

Imagery

Imagery means describing something by comparing it with a picture of something else.

When Scout refers to Atticus in court, saying 'he'd gone frog-sticking without a light' (Chapter 17), she is using a **metaphor**. She means that Atticus reminds her of someone tackling a task without the proper equipment and she conveys it by making a little picture. When she mentions 'the soft bovine sounds of the ladies' in Chapter 24, she means they sound like cows grazing — and we can imagine that. A metaphor makes the comparison by pretending that the thing or action being described actually *is* the image created.

In Chapter 12, Zeebo's voice is 'like the rumble of distant artillery' and Judge Taylor in Chapter 16 is 'like a sleepy old shark' (seemingly harmless but in reality still ready to bite). These are examples of **similes** — comparisons that use 'as' or 'like' to make it clear that two things are being likened to each other.

Scout also describes things using **personification** — describing the properties of something inanimate (without life) by pretending it has human qualities. In Chapter 1, she refers to the fence as 'a picket drunkenly [that] guarded the front yard' and the house as 'droopy and sick'.

Metaphor, simile and personification are all parts of imagery. Imagery is sometimes called 'figurative language'.

In *To Kill a Mockingbird*, the imagery is carefully drawn from the experience of children growing up in the Southern states, or from books because Scout is a compulsive reader. Harper Lee makes Scout use colourful and original images based on what would have been the experience of such a child at that place and time. 'Frog-sticking' (stabbing frogs at night that are attracted to a light in the warm, humid climate) is not likely to be a familiar game to a child in the UK today.

Harper Lee uses imagery to establish character. In Chapter 1 Scout tells us that Calpurnia's 'hand was wide as a bed slat and twice as hard'. Mayella Ewell's nervousness is stressed by Scout's description of her as 'a steady-eyed cat with a twitchy tail' (Chapter 18). Scout's repugnance at Mrs Dubose is revealed in the imagery she uses: 'Her face was the colour of a dirty pillowcase, and the corners of her mouth glistened with wet, which inched like a glacier down the deep grooves enclosing her chin' (Chapter 11).

Sometimes, Lee uses imagery to evoke a sense of place. The Ewell's home at the rubbish dump, which is very different from Scout's orderly house, is like 'the playhouse of an insane child' (Chapter 17).

Imagery is often linked to **symbolism**. For example, the mockingbird of the title is a metaphor for innocence and vulnerability, which is sustained throughout the novel (see page 48). It takes on the force of a symbol because it is woven into the whole text as a theme rather than

Grade *booster*

Be aware that *To Kill a Mockingbird* is a very carefully structured novel whose pace varies. Refer to this in your examination answers.

being mentioned once for descriptive purposes. Another example of this is Atticus's image of getting inside another person's skin and walking around in it as a metaphor for tolerance and understanding. It is central to the novel.

Language

Pause for thought

In view of what you have learned about Harper Lee's style in this section, look closely at Chapter 15 from '"Come on," whispered Jem' to "He in there, Mr Finch?" a man said.' Work out in detail the effect of her style in this passage (Jitney Jungle is a super-market chain — one of the first in the USA.)

Harper Lee uses a wide range of language styles for different purposes in *To Kill a Mockingbird* — one of the many things that makes it such an interesting and satisfying novel.

Every character, even Atticus, speaks with a broad-vowelled, slow, Southern American accent — different from the more clipped accent of, say, New York. However, on the whole, the more educated the character, the less dialect he or she uses.

Atticus uses mostly standard English and an educated vocabulary, even when speaking to his children: 'It's slipped into usage with some people like ourselves, when they want a common, ugly term to label somebody,' he tells Scout of the term 'nigger-lover' in Chapter 11. When Dill turns up unexpectedly in Chapter 14, Atticus tells him, 'And for goodness' sake put some of the county back where it belongs, the soil erosion's bad enough as it is.' Dill does not understand. It is Scout, used to her father's sense of humour, who explains, 'He's tryin' to be funny. He means take a bath.'

The children's language is more colloquial than their father's and they speak less precisely with far more **elision** (leaving out letters or syllables). For example, at the end of the novel (Chapter 31), Scout sleepily tells Atticus, 'An' they chased him 'n' never could catch him 'cause they didn't know what he looked like, an' Atticus…' It is Harper Lee's way of reminding us that this is the voice of a child.

At the same time, the children are constantly learning adult vocabulary — especially legal vocabulary — from Atticus. That is why Jem half knows what an entailment is (Chapter 2) and the adult Scout can humorously refer to the runaway Dill as 'the defendant' (Chapter 15). By the end of the novel, Jem's language is more adult than Scout's, which is another reminder that he is four years older and growing up fast.

Less educated characters, both black and white, use more dialect in their speech — words, forms of words and grammar that are not generally used in standard English such as 'chillun' for children and 'suh' for sir. A good example of dialect is Mayella Ewell saying in court (Chapter 18): 'I don't hafta take his sass, I ain't called upon to take it' — which roughly 'translated' into standard English means 'I am not obliged to put up with him [Atticus] making jokes at my expense'. Of course, in context, her meaning is absolutely clear and needs no translation. The same applies to Tom Robinson's reply to Mr Gilmer in court: 'No suh, I didn't go to be' (Chapter 19).

Harper Lee uses language as a way of defining character and creating drama. In court, Bob Ewell declares coarsely that 'I seen that black nigger yonder ruttin' on my Mayella!' (Chapter 17). This crude statement causes such shocked excitement that it takes Judge Taylor five minutes to restore order. He then instructs the witness: 'Mr Ewell, you will keep your testimony within the confines of Christian English usage, if that is possible.' Ewell's aggression in court helps to show the reader what sort of a man he really is. It prepares us for his later attack on the children.

Calpurnia's language links the educated groups in the novel with the uneducated groups. She is one of only four people at her church who can read. When the children go with her to First Purchase Church (Chapter 12), Scout is surprised to discover that Calpurnia has two ways of speaking. She adjusts to the group she is with. 'Now what if I talked white-folks' talk at church, and with my neighbours?' she tells Scout. 'They'd think I was puttin' on airs to beat Moses.' Calpurnia is thus presented as being wise, tolerant and adaptable, unlike many Maycomb people.

There are jokes with language in the novel to show that characters are failing fully to understand. Scout uses the word 'morphodite' in Chapter 8 for example. She means 'hermaphrodite' — a creature like her snowman with both male and female characteristics. Bob Ewell does not know the meaning of 'ambidextrous' — able to use right and left hand equally well — and therefore contradicts himself in court (Chapter 17).

The word 'nigger' occurs frequently in *To Kill a Mockingbird*. It comes from the Latin word *niger*, meaning 'black'. Gradually, 'nigger' has become a term of offensive racist abuse. It was a little more acceptable in the 1930s than it is now, although Atticus tells Scout not to use it because it is 'common'. Notice that the black people in the novel use it of themselves too. At First Purchase Church, Calpurnia addresses Lula as 'nigger'. Harper Lee, writing in the late 1950s, never uses it directly. She says 'coloured'. You will undoubtedly need to use the word 'nigger' or 'nigger-lover' in your essays. Put inverted commas around these terms to show you are quoting other people's words.

Review your learning

1 What basic story-telling method does Harper Lee use in *To Kill a Mockingbird*?

2 What are the limitations of this method and how does she get around them?

3 What does the novel gain from its setting?

4 For what purposes does Harper Lee use imagery? List as many different uses as you can, giving examples.

5 Why does Harper Lee make Mr Cunningham speak differently from Uncle Jack? List some examples.

 More interactive questions and answers online.

Tackling the exam

- **What sort of questions will you have to answer in the exam?**
- **How can you plan your answers?**
- **What is the best way to start and finish essays?**
- **How should you use quotations?**
- **What do you have to do to get an A*?**

Different forms of assessment

Although all GCSE assessment is similar, the details of what you have to do vary according to which examining board your school or centre uses for English Literature. *To Kill a Mockingbird* is a text set by OCR, WJEC, AQA, Edexcel and CCEA. If you do not know, find out from your teachers which board you will be, or are, entered with.

OCR

OCR assesses *To Kill a Mockingbird* in Unit 3: Prose from Different Cultures. It is a 45-minute exam paper and you are expected to take your copy of the novel into the exam with you. You must pick one task (or question) from a choice of three. One of these three is passage-based. That means that you are given, or referred to, an extract of the novel and asked to write about it in relation to the whole novel. The other two tasks require you to write essays.

WJEC

WJEC assesses *To Kill a Mockingbird* in Unit 1 Section A: Different Cultures Prose. The work on *To Kill a Mockingbird* is the first half of a two-hour exam paper so you have one hour to spend on it. You may *not* take your copy of the novel in with you. You must answer two questions, the first of which is compulsory and passage-based. There are two options to choose from for the second essay-style question.

AQA

AQA assesses *To Kill a Mockingbird* in Unit 1: Exploring Modern Texts: Exploring Cultures. The work on *To Kill a Mockingbird* is the first half of a 1 hour 30 minute paper so you have 45 minutes to spend on it. You are expected to take your copy of the novel into the exam with you. There is one passage-based task only — no choice. That means that you are given, or referred to, an extract of the novel and are required to write about it in relation to the whole novel.

Edexcel

Edexcel GCSE English Literature assesses *To Kill a Mockingbird* in Unit 1: Understanding Prose. If you are with Edexcel your teachers may have decided that you will also use the same text for part of your GCSE English Language assessment. For English Language Edexcel assesses *To Kill a Mockingbird* in Unit 2: The Writer's Voice.

The English Literature work on *To Kill a Mockingbird* is the second half of a 1 hour 45 minute paper. You are expected to take a copy of the novel — which must have nothing written in it — into the exam with you. You must choose one of two tasks. The first is a four-part question based on a passage. You must also show your knowledge of the rest of the novel. The alternative task is an essay with pointers to guide you.

The English Language work on *To Kill a Mockingbird* consists of a 500-word provided passage from the novel — the first half of a 1 hour 45 minute paper. You may *not* take the text into the exam for this paper. You are expected to write about voice, imagery, appeal to the senses, speech and thought, techniques of persuasion, sentence length and variety, structure and any other interesting use of language. There is a great deal in this guide to help you with this, especially in the section on *Style* (pages 53–59).

> ### Key quotation
>
> **'I wanted you to see what real courage is, instead of getting the idea that courage is a man with a gun in his hand. It's when you know you're licked before you begin but you begin anyway and you see it through no matter what.'**
>
> (Atticus, Chapter 11)

CCEA

CCEA assesses *To Kill a Mockingbird* in Unit 1: The Study of Prose. The exam lasts 1 hour and you must answer one question on the novel from a choice of two. You may *not* take a copy of the novel with you, as this is a closed-book exam. If you answer a passage-based question, the extract will be printed on the exam paper.

Higher and foundation tiers

All the boards set their English Literature GCSE exams at higher and foundation tiers. If you take the higher tier you can get grades A*–D (with the possibility of an E). If you take the foundation tier you can get grades C–G. You and your teachers (and probably parents) will decide which is the more suitable level for you.

Higher-tier candidates are provided with a question (or task) and expected to work out for themselves how to structure an answer. If you

are entered for the higher tier with OCR, WJEC, Edexcel or CCEA you will be asked essay questions like these in the exam:

1 Atticus told Scout, 'You never really know a man until you stand in his shoes and walk around in them.' What has Scout learned about life from other people's perspectives by the end of the novel?

2 Explain why you think Harper Lee called her novel *To Kill a Mockingbird*.

3 The novel is narrated by a child. What are the advantages and disadvantages of this way of telling a story?

4 How do the characters of Jem and Scout change and mature during the novel?

5 How is the theme of racial prejudice presented in *To Kill a Mockingbird*?

6 Examine the ways in which Harper Lee presents the black community.

Foundation-tier candidates with OCR, WJEC, Edexcel or CCEA will be given essay tasks like these. The bullet points below each question suggest an outline framework for the answer:

1 Is Mayella Ewell a victim to feel sorry for or someone to despise because she accuses an innocent man? In your answer comment on:
- what Mayella says in court
- what Tom Robinson and Bob Ewell say in court, prompted by Atticus
- what others say about the Ewell family elsewhere in the novel

2 How far do you agree that Atticus is an ideal father and citizen? Your answer should consider:
- Atticus's reaction to Scout, Jem and Dill playing games about Boo Radley at the beginning of the novel
- the mad dog episode
- occasions when Atticus talks to his children
- his treatment of Mrs Dubose
- his behaviour at the trial of Tom Robinson
- his attitude to Bob Ewell's threatening behaviour after the trial

3 What different sorts of courage are shown in *To Kill a Mockingbird*? Include in your answer what you think about:
- the children's approaches to Boo Radley and his reactions
- the shooting of the mad dog
- Mrs Dubose giving up morphine
- Atticus standing up for justice
- Mr Cunningham turning away from the jail
- Boo Radley killing Bob Ewell

And here is an example of a passage-based task set as an alternative to an essay by OCR, WJEC and Edexcel and as the only option by AQA and CCEA (CCEA offers a choice of two questions based on the same passage):

Read from 'By the time we reached our front steps Walter had forgotten he was a Cunningham' (Chapter 3, about one page in from the beginning) to '"She likes Jem better'n me anyway" I concluded and suggested that Atticus lose no time in packing her off.'

At higher tier the question might be:

How does Harper Lee portray the relationship between Scout and Calpurnia here?

At foundation tier the question might be:

What do you think makes the relationship between Scout and Calpurnia so fascinating here? You should consider:
- what Scout says and does
- what Calpurnia says and does
- the words and phrases Harper Lee uses

Edexcel says — and this is likely to apply to all boards — that foundation-tier questions will focus on key events in the novel, character and theme while higher-tier questions will focus on character, theme and the significance of the passage you are given to the rest of the novel.

Tackling the tasks

Remember:
- English literature does not have right and wrong answers.
- No two answers, even if they score the same marks, will contain exactly the same material.
- You can answer a question in more than one way and still score high marks.
- All your points must be supported by evidence (quotations or reference to events) from the novel.
- You must do more than retell the story: your job is to demonstrate your knowledge and understanding by commenting on the novel.
- The examiner is interested in your response to *To Kill a Mockingbird* and what you think about it.

There are three main sorts of question — plot, character and theme focused — which you are likely to be asked at GCSE. Here are some examples:

Atticus told Scout, 'You never really know a man until you stand in his shoes and walk around in them.' What has Scout learned about life from other people's perspectives by the end of the novel?

Pause for thought

As a revision exercise, go through the six higher-tier questions on page 62 and suggest the bullet-point guidance you would expect to see if they were offered at the foundation tier. This is a useful activity whichever tier you are entered for.

As you can see, higher-tier and foundation-tier questions are similar. The main difference is that foundation-tier candidates receive guidance about how to tackle the question.

The question on page 63 focuses on the plot — what happens in the novel and how Harper Lee makes it interesting.

How do the characters of Jem and Scout change and mature during the novel?

The question above asks you to think about characters and how Harper Lee presents them.

How is the theme of racial prejudice presented in *To Kill a Mockingbird*?

This question asks you to unravel and analyse a major Harper Lee theme.

Planning your answers

Always work out what the question is asking you to do and make a plan before you begin. In an exam, when you are under time pressure, you will have to do this quickly. First, use a highlighter to emphasise the key words in the question, or you could underline them.

Then devise an essay plan — even two or three minutes spent making a plan will pay off. Your answer will be better thought out, better shaped and you are less likely to miss out important points if you have noted them in your plan. This could make the difference between getting a C or D grade and a B, A or A*.

Experiment with different sorts of plan and decide what works for you. Some people like diagrammatic plans. This usually means putting the key idea in a circle in the middle of the page and adding points for inclusion, linked to the key idea, around the outside. Alternatively, make a list and number the points. Below is a plan for the following question.

Atticus told Scout, 'You never really know a man until you stand in his shoes and walk around in them.' What has Scout learned about life from other people's perspectives by the end of the novel?

1 Introduction: Atticus makes this comment about Boo. It also applies to Bob E, Mrs D, Aunt A.
2 Boo — Scout's main lesson from tormenting in Ch 1 to complete understanding at end. Radley porch = symbol.
3 Bob E vicious and lazy — Scout knows no one else like this. Understands eventually he's better dead. Sympathy for Mayella through trial.
4 Mrs D seems spiteful until Scout learns otherwise.
5 Aunt A friction with Scout at first. S gradually develops respect for her point of view — she's right about Bob E.
6 Conclusion: novel could be subtitled 'What Scout Learns'. HL details S's mental development age 6–9 and uses incidents to shape it.

Always 'frame' your answer with an introduction and a conclusion. You are unlikely to be able to make more than four main points in the body of your answer in the time available to you in the exam.

Try to plan your time carefully so that you always complete your answer. However, if you misjudge the time and do not finish, hand in your plan so that the examiner can see where your answer was going.

The sample plan above is, of course, not the only way that this question could be answered. As a revision exercise, devise a plan of your own for a different answer to this question. You might include, for example, what Scout learns about the black community through visiting Calpurnia's church and from hearing Dill's account of Atticus's call on Mrs Robinson to tell her that Tom is dead. Another possibility would be to exclude Mrs Dubose and to bring in a discussion of what Scout learns from, and through, Miss Maudie Atkinson, Nathan Radley, Mr Cunningham and/or Dolphus Raymond.

> ### *Key quotation*
>
> **Thus began our longest journey together.**
>
> (Scout, Chapter 27)

You may prefer to create a mini-mind map or spider diagram as your essay plan — especially if you are a visual learner. Suppose you are asked the question 'How does Lee present the education of Scout and others in *To Kill a Mockingbird*? Your sketch might look something like this:

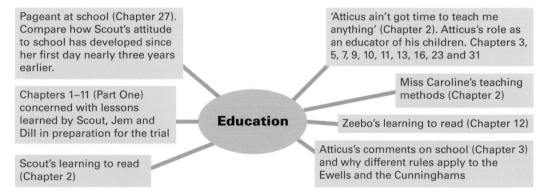

- Pageant at school (Chapter 27). Compare how Scout's attitude to school has developed since her first day nearly three years earlier.
- Chapters 1–11 (Part One) concerned with lessons learned by Scout, Jem and Dill in preparation for the trial
- Scout's learning to read (Chapter 2)
- **Education**
- 'Atticus ain't got time to teach me anything' (Chapter 2). Atticus's role as an educator of his children. Chapters 3, 5, 7, 9, 10, 11, 13, 16, 23 and 31
- Miss Caroline's teaching methods (Chapter 2)
- Zeebo's learning to read (Chapter 12)
- Atticus's comments on school (Chapter 3) and why different rules apply to the Ewells and the Cunninghams

Essay openings

You will get no marks for copying the question in your opening sentence or paragraph. Instead, your introduction might:

- say how you are going to tackle the question
- interpret the question — say what you think it means
- comment on something that is in the question
- make some general introductory remarks

The examiner's aim is to seek out mark-scoring parts of your essay. You will score marks for making informed analytical comments. Do not waste your limited time writing anything else.

Below are four possible introductions for an essay answering the following question:

How do the characters of Jem and Scout change and mature during the novel?

Introduction 1

Both Scout and Jem develop during the course of the novel as they work their way through various incidents and experiences. In this essay, I shall focus on three major factors: their growing understanding of Boo Radley, what they learn about human nature through the trial of Tom Robinson and the influence Atticus has on them.

Introduction 2

This question suggests that Harper Lee has built into the novel a developmental path for Scout and Jem. I agree that she has shown the children growing up and the changes that it brings, although I believe that she presents it more strongly for Jem than for Scout, as I shall show.

Introduction 3

The key word in this question is 'change'. One of Harper Lee's great achievements in *To Kill a Mockingbird* is not only to get right into Scout's mind so that the reader always understands how it feels to be frightened of Boo Radley, admiring of Miss Maudie and so on, but to take us on a journey through growing up. The six-year-old Scout we meet at the beginning of the novel is very different from the maturing nine-year-old we leave on the last page. Through Scout's viewpoint, Harper Lee shows us Jem's shift into adolescence too.

> **Key quotation**
>
> 'Atticus Finch won't win, he can't win, but he's the only man in these parts who can keep a jury out so long in a case like that. And I thought to myself, well, we're making a step — it's just a baby-step, but it's a step.'
>
> (Miss Maudie, Chapter 22)

Introduction 4

Scout starts the novel as a child of six who is led by her elder brother and their friend Dill into a childishly irrational fear of Boo Radley. Three years later, when the novel ends, she has spoken to Boo, stood on his porch (in his 'shoes') and recognised the moving truth about him. Jem, meanwhile, has progressed from a less-than-thoughtful ten-year-old to a perceptive young man of 13, acutely interested in law and justice. Harper Lee has brought about these changes by taking the children through a series of experiences.

Essay endings

You will get no extra marks for repeating in your conclusion something that you have said already. In your conclusion, you might:

- summarise your arguments and draw them together in a new way
- make a new point, which you have deliberately held back for the ending
- try to be 'punchy' so that there is a sense of an essay that has been finished rather than just tailing off

Below are three possible conclusions for an essay answering the following question.

How do the characters of Jem and Scout change and mature during the novel?

Conclusion 1

Harper Lee has shown us Scout and Jem being curious about Boo, learning the deceptive truth about Mrs Dubose, and seeing, at first hand during the trial of Tom Robinson, that justice is not fairly applied in 1930s Alabama. Because the author presents them in a range of situations and lets us see and hear them in conversation with wise people like Atticus, Miss Maudie and Dolphus Raymond, we appreciate that, as they change and mature, these children are the hope for Maycomb's future.

Conclusion 2

Scout, who ends the novel thinking back to the child who once stopped at an oak tree 'delighted, puzzled, apprehensive', feels 'very old' and assumes that there is not much more for her and Jem to learn 'except possibly algebra'. Of course she is wrong, and the adult Scout, decades later, is smiling at her younger self. Nonetheless, three years is a long time in the life of a child and Harper Lee has shown us how both children have been changed by, for example, watching the trial, learning to live with their aunt and experiencing the horror of being attacked.

Conclusion 3

To Kill a Mockingbird ends where it began. Jem's arm is 'badly broken at the elbow' and the children have reached a temporary stopping place on a three-year learning curve. Both now know much more about human nature than they did three years earlier, thanks to Tom Robinson, Bob Ewell and Boo Radley, among others.

Using evidence in essays

Just as scientists provide evidence to back up their theories, you need to provide evidence to back up the points in your essay. All the evidence you require lies within the covers of *To Kill a Mockingbird*.

There are two types of evidence:

- Quotation of exact words written in the novel. Look for short phrases that illustrate your point and weave them into your sentences. Always remember to include quotation marks. You should not need to quote more than one sentence at a time. Aim to work at least eight direct quotations into an exam essay. Structure your sentences like these examples:

Once Jem is 12, Scout finds him 'inconsistent' and 'moody', but Calpurnia, ever perceptive, tells her not to 'fret too much' because the maturing Jem will need to be 'off to himself' and 'doin' whatever boys do'.

As Harper Lee builds up the tension, Scout suddenly realises that their 'company' in the wood has 'shuffled and dragged his feet' before she hears him 'running towards us with no child's steps'.

- Reference to incidents in the novel without quoting directly. You might mention, for example, Lula's attitude to Scout and Jem at First Purchase Church (Chapter 12) as an example of reverse racism without quoting the exact words said. Alternatively, you could mention Heck Tate's deference to Atticus as the better shot when the rabid dog needs killing quickly and efficiently in Chapter 10 as an example of the respect Atticus commands in the community.

Essay writing: five tips

- Write as fully as you can but be selective and focus on detail.
- Make a quick plan before you start. Aim to make five or six key points and manage your time carefully, which includes leaving yourself a few minutes at the end to check your work.
- Back up your statements with evidence from the novel.
- Spell and punctuate accurately — especially the names of characters or places in the novel.
- Use formal English and avoid slang and colloquialisms.

...and five don'ts

- Don't retell the story.
- Don't waste your time writing out long quotations that are not grafted tightly into your arguments.
- Don't begin sentences or paragraphs with 'The above quotation shows...'.
- Don't try to write everything you know about *To Kill a Mockingbird*.
- Don't confuse Harper Lee, the author of *To Kill a Mockingbird*, with Scout, her fictional narrator.

Assessment Objectives and skills

All GCSE examinations are pinned to very specific areas of learning that the examiners want to be sure that candidates have mastered. These are known as Assessment Objectives or AOs.

Think of AOs as dartboard-like targets or like the ones on a shooting range. The examiner is watching the target. You aim for it. You get marks if you hit it but not if you don't — and, in general, the more direct your hit the more marks you are likely you get.

There are four AOs for GCSE English Literature but only three that relate to your work on *To Kill a Mockingbird*. You cannot, of course, divide learning of this sort into neat self-contained chunks so the AOs overlap.

In essence this is what the AOs are, although each of the four boards uses slightly different wording:

- **AO1:** (Candidates must) respond critically and imaginatively and select and evaluate relevant textual detail to illustrate and support interpretations.
- **AO2:** (Candidates must) explain how language, structure and form contribute to the writer's presentation of ideas, themes and settings.
- **AO4:** (Candidates must) relate texts to their social, cultural and historical contexts and explain how texts have been influential to self and other readers in significant contexts and at different times.

The examining boards share out their attention to AOs in slightly different ways.

AO	Exam board
AO1	AQA, WJEC, Edexcel, CCEA
AO2	AQA, WJEC, OCR, CCEA
AO4	OCR, Edexcel

So what do these rather complicated AO statements mean, and what are examiners really looking for?

AO1

You are required (by AQA, WJEC, Edexcel and CCEA) to show that you have read the book carefully and thought about it from a number of angles.

'Imaginatively and critically' means two separate things. First you need to have travelled to Maycomb in your mind, considered how Scout, Atticus, Tom Robinson and other characters must have felt, and thought carefully about why. (You could call this 'standing in their shoes' as Atticus does!) That is imaginative reading. But of course to meet this AO, not only do you have to read imaginatively, you have to be able to write about your reading in order to demonstrate its imaginativeness.

Critical reading is a different skill. It involves being aware of why Harper Lee makes the decisions that she does. Why, for instance, does she make Scout the narrator and not Jem or Atticus? Would it have been a better or worse novel if she had told the story differently? What use does she make of 'lesser characters' such as Miss Maudie, Mrs Dubose and Link Deas? Why are they in the novel and what is their purpose? Some answers to these questions are suggested in earlier sections of this guide. If you show that you are aware of such questions and able to offer some ideas to answer them in your exam essays, you will be demonstrating 'critical' reading and meeting the AO1 target.

One way of making sure that you write 'critically' is to use the author's name or refer to her as often as you can. Make statements, beginning, for instance:

Harper Lee makes us aware…
Lee presents…
The author makes it clear that…
Harper Lee evidently sympathises with…
Lee makes Scout say…
Lee tells us through Scout…
Harper Lee wants the reader to know that…

Remember — and this is the second part of AO1 — that every point (or 'interpretation') you make must be supported with 'relevant textual detail'. That means that you use brief quotations or you refer to incidents in the text as evidence to support what you are saying. Suppose, for instance, you are writing about the way in which Jem grows up and away from Scout during the course of *To Kill a Mockingbird*. You might write the following — note how carefully the five items of relevant textual detail, or evidence, are woven in:

> **Key quotation**
>
> **The rifle cracked. Tim Johnson leaped, flopped over and crumpled on the sidewalk in a brown-and-white heap. He didn't know what hit him.**
>
> (Scout, Chapter 10)

Scout tells us in Chapter 6, when Jem goes to get his trousers, that 'Jem and I began to part company'. During the compelled visits to Mrs Dubose (Chapter 11) Scout notices her brother acquiring 'an alien set of values'. Later, in Chapter 12, Jem advises Scout to be more respectful of their aunt by 'bein' a girl and acting right'. In Chapter 14, he breaks 'the remaining code of our childhood' by going to tell Atticus about Dill's secret arrival in the Finch house. It is also at about this time that Calpurnia starts to treat Jem as an adult by addressing him as 'Mister Jem'. Jem has come a long way since the childish Boo Radley games in the first few chapters of the novel.

Here is another example. Suppose you are writing about the role of Calpurnia in *To Kill a Mockingbird*. The first sentence makes a statement. The second offers three pieces of 'relevant textual detail' to support it.

Harper Lee uses Calpurnia as a link between the white and black communities. For example, in Chapter 12, it is through her that Scout learns more about the difficulties faced by the Robinson family. Atticus asks her, in Chapter 22, to thank the black community for their gifts to him and it is Calpurnia whom Atticus asks, in Chapter 24, to accompany him when he goes to tell Helen Robinson that her husband Tom has been shot.

Memorise the main points of the AOs your examining board is using for the work on *To Kill a Mockingbird*. Keep them in your mind — or jot them down in note form on rough paper to keep beside you — as you plan and write your essays. Remember that whichever board's exam you are doing, only two AOs (see table on page 69) will apply. Make sure that you hit the bullseye on the imaginary target by giving the examiner plenty of both AOs.

AO2

This AO (for AQA, WJEC, OCR and CCEA) requires you to show that you understand not just *what* Harper Lee has written in *To Kill a Mockingbird* but *how* she has used her writer's tools. Like all authors, Lee has used language very precisely for specific purposes and she has chosen to shape her novel to tell her story in a particular way. 'Language, structure and form' cover things such as:

- Lee's use of an invisible adult narrator looking back on her childhood and therefore able to use adult language (see 'Viewpoint', page 53).
- her use of dialect to suggest the Southern states setting and to distinguish between educated and less educated characters, particularly white and black (see 'Language', pages 58–59).

Grade *booster*

You should know *To Kill a Mockingbird* very well indeed by the time you take your examination. However, you will not be able to write everything you know about it in your answer. The skill is to select from the information you know in order to answer the specific question that is set. This is why planning is so important.

- the division of the novel into two parts (see timeline on pages 26–27 and 'Structure', pages 27–29).
- the climax (the trial) followed by a second climax (Ewell's attack on Scout and Jem) (see 'Structure', pages 27–29).

To meet AO2 you also need to show how Lee uses these 'tools' to tell her story and to convey the messages she wants to get across to the reader. This is what is meant by her 'presentation of ideas, themes and settings'.

For example, if you were writing about the trial and Lee's presentation of Tom Robinson, this passage might form part of your essay:

Tom Robinson, 'a black-velvet Negro, not shiny, but soft black velvet' (Chapter 19), is presented as a hard-working cotton picker employed by Link Deas. He is a kindly, family man. Lee shows us — through his testimony at the trial — how he makes time to help Mayella after work because he feels sorry for her (Chapter 20). Later, it is reported to Scout by Dill that Tom's wife faints with shock when she learns of his death (Chapter 25). We learn that his children are polite and well cared for (Chapter 20). He has much more in common with Atticus than the white Bob Ewell, and Lee shows us, rather than tells us, this by giving us all this information about him so that we are led to draw our own conclusions — part of the way she structures *To Kill a Mockingbird* so that we, like Scout, learn as the novel proceeds.

In Chapter 20, Tom speaks politely and respectfully to the court and is reluctant to describe Mayella's lonely sexual approach to him. As Scout comments in Chapter 19, 'It occurred to me that in their own way, Tom Robinson's manners were as good as Atticus's'. In the incident with Mayella, Tom could not win. Had he turned 'ugly' by pushing or striking her, he would have been arrested for assaulting a white woman, so he ran away instead: 'A sure sign of guilt' (Chapter 20).

Tom Robinson, whose tragedy is at the centre of the novel, is presented as an ideal black man and someone against whom the reader can measure other characters. Harper Lee unravels the story in a way which makes us feel that Tom's trial and death are deeply regrettable, although there is hope for other black people in a similar position in the future because of the sympathy evoked for Tom by Atticus and others. He is, like Boo Radley, a 'mockingbird'. He harms no one — and therefore does not deserve to die — is Lee's clear conclusion.

All three paragraphs would score examiner's ticks for AO2.
- The first paragraph concentrates on Lee's method — description of his appearance, account of his relationship with others — of conveying Tom's appearance and character to the reader, some of it first-hand observation by Scout (in court) and some of it what she has been told by others.

- The second paragraph refers to the way Tom speaks and shares Scout's thoughts about his manners, showing how Lee's use of, and focus on, language contributes to character development and the reader's understanding of it.
- The third paragraph points out that Tom's tragedy is the central event within the structure of *To Kill a Mockingbird* and relates him to one of the novel's main themes — mockingbirds — an important strand in the novel.

> **Key quotation**
>
> 'A mob's always made up of people, no matter what. Mr Cunningham was part of a mob last night, but he was still a man.'
>
> (Atticus, Chapter 16)

AO4

Examining the context of a novel involves seeing the situation it presents in comparison with situations at other times and in other places — this is discussed in detail in the *Context* section of this guide.

In brief, the historical context of *To Kill a Mockingbird* is that it is set in 1930s Alabama against a background of racial tension and the economic depression which was affecting the whole of America and much of rest of the world.

Its social context is its treatment of different races and social classes and they way they react together or against each other — often compared (through Uncle Jack's and Link Deas's children) with different attitudes in the North.

To Kill a Mockingbird's cultural context is the tight insularity of the Maycomb way of life. It is rather cut off from the outside world and few of its inhabitants have travelled far — as Scout often reminds us. Many (Miss Stephanie Crawford, Nathan Radley, Lula and many more) are very set in their ways and views and cannot imagine life beyond Maycomb.

Of course, these three aspects of context — social, cultural and historical — are closely related to each other and there is a lot of overlap. The important thing to remember is that you have to bear the context in mind as you read, study and write about *To Kill a Mockingbird*. You cannot make sense of the novel without it.

When you are writing, it makes sense occasionally to use the words 'social context', 'cultural context' and 'historical context', or something similar, to show the examiner that you are fulfilling AO4. For example, if you were answering a question about Atticus's role at the trial you might write:

He is asked by Judge Taylor to take on the Tom Robinson rape case because only Atticus, the judge knows, would make a serious attempt to defend a black man — a clear illustration of the social context in an insular, racist, 1930s Alabama small

town. Although Atticus knows his children will suffer (racist) taunts because of it, he believes he must take on the case. He is a gently (not bigoted) religious man and to him it is a matter of conscience and self-respect. 'If I didn't I couldn't hold up my head in town, I couldn't represent this county in the legislature, I couldn't even tell you or Jem not to do something again,' he tells Scout in Chapter 9, adding that 'every lawyer gets at least one case in his lifetime that affects him personally. This one's mine, I guess.' Here Lee is showing us how Atticus's social class and education drives his actions — just as Bob Ewell's lack of social standing, education and integrity drive his. It is part of her presentation of the culture of Maycomb as it would have been in the economically troubled 1930s.

Sample essays

Question 1 (higher tier: OCR, WJEC or AQA)

To what extent is Atticus presented as a good father and citizen?

Grade C essay

Atticus Finch's wife has died. Scout, who is telling the story, tells the reader a lot about her father, a single parent. [1] She mentions his faults too. 'Atticus was feeble: he was nearly fifty,' **(AO1)** she says before describing the mad dog incident. Then she says that he wears glasses. 'He did not do the things our schoolmates' fathers did: he never went hunting, he did not play poker or drink or smoke. He sat in the living-room and read.' **(AO1)**

Scout is an exact contempry [2] of Harper Lee, the author. Lee's father, like Atticus, was an Alabama lawyer. Harper Lee is probably writing a bit of [3] autobiography and creating an ideal father and citizen. [4] **(AO4)**

Jem chops down Mrs Dubose's camellias because he is distressed after the old lady says Atticus is 'lawing for niggers'. **(AO1)** Atticus tells off Jem and sends him alone to apologise. Another time, Atticus makes Scout apologise to Aunt Alexandra for rudeness: 'as long as your aunt's in the house you do as she tells you,' he says.

Yet most of the time he is warm and there for Scout. [5] 'I ran to Atticus for comfort,' Scout says [6] after being smacked by Uncle Jack for fighting with her cousin Francis. **(AO1)** When Jem returns from apologising to Mrs Dubose, Scout is having a cuddle with her dad. [7]

Atticus is wise as a father too, which Harper Lee shows us. He tells them what 'compromise' and 'entailment' mean. **(AO2)** He talks to the children about his work and makes them understand why he has to defend Tom Robinson.

He says 'when you and Jem are grown, maybe you'll look back on this with some compassion and some feeling that I didn't let you down. This case, Tom Robinson's case, is something that goes to the essence of a man's conscience — Scout, I couldn't go to church and worship God if I didn't try to help that man'. [8] This quotation shows that Atticus is a good father and a good citizen.

1 Strong introduction

2 Spelling mistake
3 Colloquialism
4 Shows understanding of context

5 Colloquialism
6 Good use of evidence
7 Colloquialism

8 Quotation too long

However, Atticus has different ideas to Aunt Alexandra. In Chapter 13, Atticus cannot explain Maycomb's 'caste system' **(AO4)** to the children as his sister wants him to. The children know the adults are dissagreeing [9] about this, but Atticus will not side with them against their aunt. We can see another side of Atticus in the way he relates to his sister. [10]

9 Spelling mistake
10 Perceptive comments

Outside the home, Atticus is a proper Christian. **(AO4)** Judge Taylor knows that. That is why he asks Atticus to defend Tom Robinson so that he has a chance of a fair trial. [11]

11 Incisive 'punchy' style

We also see how much Miss Maudie Atkinson and the black community **(AO4)** like Atticus and think he is a good citizen. Miss Maudie says 'We're so rarely called on to be Christians, but when we are, we've got men like Atticus to go for us.' When Atticus goes with Calpurnia (and Jem and Dill, who later describes it to Scout) to break the news of Tom's death to Helen Robinson, we see that the black people respect him too. Reverend Sykes gets the black people in the gallery at the end of the trial to stand up in homage to Atticus. That's another example. [12]

12 Clumsy expression

Yet not everyone thinks Atticus is a good guy. [13] Atticus says **(AO2)** 'it's a sin to kill a mockingbird' [14] — meaning innocent people like Boo Radley and Tom Robinson — but he knows sometimes dangerous things have to be killed. That is why he shoots the dog. In the end, Bob Ewell dies too. [15]

13 Colloquialism
14 Quotation not linked to useful point
15 Points set down without a strong argument linking them together

Bob Ewell is a bad father and bad citizen. He is not like Atticus. Atticus makes a big mistake about him. He gets it seriously wrong about how dangerous Bob Ewell is to the Finches. This time, Aunt Alexandra is right. Atticus says Ewell 'got it all out of his system that morning' (when he spat tobaco [16] juice all over Atticus in the post office). So, Atticus is not perfect. [17]

16 Spelling mistake
17 Good analysis

At the end, Harper Lee shows us **(AO2)** Atticus being a devoted father. He is shocked because Jem is hurt and he thinks it is his fault. He will not leave his son's bedside although at the same time he helps Scout to understand about the real Boo Radley. He does not want to cover up what Boo has done either, so that shows he is a good citizen. He only agrees because Heck Tate will not take no for an answer. [18]

18 Points set down without a strong argument linking them together

Atticus is meant to be a really good man, both with his children and with the people in the town, as I have tried to show. [19]

19 Reasonable conclusion

This essay answers the question and there is some material relating to each AO. But it is carelessly written and many of the points are not taken as far as they could be.

Grade A* essay

Atticus Finch, a single parent since the death of his wife four years before the main action of the novel begins, is presented entirely from Scout's point of view. **(AO2)**

She, of course, sees her father in a childlike manner and notices his faults as well as his virtues because she is so close to him. 'Atticus was feeble: he was nearly fifty,' [1] she says before describing the mad dog incident, going on to tell the reader that he wore glasses and did nothing glamorous or exciting such as 'drive a dump-truck'. **(AO1)**

Scout is an exact contemporary of her creator, Harper Lee, whose own father, like Atticus, was an Alabama lawyer. Harper Lee is probably using her own experience to present her ideal father and citizen. [2] **(AO4)**

For example, Atticus is presented as firm but fair with his children. When Jem chops down Mrs Dubose's camellias because he is distressed by her condemnation of Atticus 'lawing for niggers', [3] Atticus reprimands Jem in a voice 'like the winter wind' [3] and sends him alone to apologise. On another occasion, Atticus, his voice 'deadly', insists that Scout apologise to Aunt Alexandra for rudeness: 'as long as your aunt's in the house you do as she tells you,' he says. [3] **(AO1)**

Yet most of the time he is warmly affectionate. 'I ran to Atticus for comfort,' Harper Lee has Scout say **(AO2)** after being smacked by Uncle Jack for fighting with her cousin Francis. When Jem returns from apologising to Mrs Dubose 'he found me still in Atticus's lap' and in the autumn, after the trial, when she tries to climb into her father's lap, he smiles and says 'You're getting so big now, I'll just have to hold a part of you.'

Harper Lee shows us Atticus's wisdom as a father too. He explains the meaning of words such as 'compromise' and 'entailment'. **(AO2)** He talks to the children about his work and makes them understand why he has to defend Tom Robinson. He lets them learn from their mistakes. Scout later realises, for example, that Atticus knew at the time that she, Jem and Dill were trying to attract Boo Radley's attention with their games. When Jem asks why there are no women on juries, he says 'I was wondering when that'd occur to you'. **(AO4)**

However, Atticus's values and views **(AO4)** are often different from Aunt Alexandra's, and Harper Lee wants the reader to notice these contrasts. In Chapter 13, the author makes comedy out of Atticus's failure to explain Maycomb's 'caste system' to the children as his sister wants him to. The children are well aware that their father and aunt do not agree about this but, nonetheless, Atticus refuses to side with them against their aunt, who anyway becomes a softer, more sympathetic character after the trial is lost and Tom Robinson is dead. **(AO1)** Atticus's relationship with his sister is another way in which Lee presents us with Atticus as a complex character, both father and citizen, whom we see in a range of contexts. **(AO4)**

1 Short quotation

2 Extended introduction that makes mark-scoring points and refers closely to text as well as opening the essay

3 Short quotations all incorporated within sentences

Outside the home, Atticus, a true Christian, **(AO4)** is specifically asked to defend Tom Robinson by Judge Taylor. He agrees because, as he tells Scout, 'I couldn't go to church and worship God if I didn't try to help that man'. **(AO2)** Judge Taylor respects Atticus's commitment to equality and justice so much that he knows that if Atticus defends him, Tom Robinson stands some chance of a fair trial.

4 Accurate use of vocabulary

We also see the high esteem [4] in which Atticus is held as a citizen through the conversations Lee presents the children having with Miss Maudie Atkinson and through the respect he attracts from the black community. **(AO2)** 'We're so rarely called on to be Christians, but when we are, we've got men like Atticus to go for us,' Miss Maudie tells the children. That respect and admiration is palpable [4] too when Atticus goes with Calpurnia (and Jem and Dill, who later describes it to Scout) to break the news of Tom's death to Helen Robinson. **(AO2)** Reverend Sykes bringing the black population to its feet in silent homage [4] to Atticus at the end of the trial is another example.

Yet that admiration of Atticus's citizenship is not universal. While Atticus is adamant that 'it's a sin to kill a mockingbird' — meaning people like Boo Radley and Tom Robinson — because they do nothing but 'sing', he also accepts that there are some elements in society which need to be removed for the safety of the majority. **(AO4)** The rabid dog, which Atticus shoots, is one example. Bob Ewell is another. **(AO2)**

Bob Ewell, unlike Atticus, is a bad father and bad citizen. He is Atticus's big error of judgement. Although normally a good judge of human behaviour, Atticus seriously underestimates the danger of Bob Ewell to the Finch family. On this occasion, Aunt Alexandra is right and Atticus is wrong. His view of human nature is too accommodating. **(AO1)** After being spat at in the post office, Atticus concludes of Ewell that he 'got it all out of his system that morning'. In this way, Harper Lee makes sure the characterisation of Atticus is fully rounded. He is a good father and citizen but he is also human and capable of mistakes. [5]

5 Events interpreted, not just recounted

At the end of the novel, Harper Lee shows us Atticus being a devoted father. Horrified by the danger that has injured Jem — for which Atticus blames himself — he is reluctant to leave his son's bedside, although at the same time he educates Scout about the real Boo Radley. **(AO1)** We also see him still striving to be a good citizen. Only reluctantly does he agree to cover up Boo Radley's (justified) killing of Bob Ewell, and while he still believes it was Jem who wielded the knife in self-defence he will not hear of it. He is depicted as a man of total integrity and certainly as a good father and citizen, as I have tried to show. **(AO1)** We have to remember, however, that — because of the way the novel is structured and narrated — he is also the most fully developed father and citizen in the novel, so our knowledge of him is deeper than it is of the other fathers and citizens it presents. [6] **(AO2)**

6 Extended conclusion that makes mark-scoring points and refers closely to text as well as concluding the essay; emphasis on Harper Lee's achievement

78

Overall, the question is fully answered and referred to in every paragraph. It covers AO1, AO2 and AO4 adequately. The essay is well expressed and free from spelling mistakes.

Question 2 (higher tier: OCR, WJEC or AQA)

The trial of Tom Robinson is a clear example of racial prejudice at work. Examine the different forms of prejudice that occur in the novel. How has Harper Lee made her own views about prejudice clear?

> **Key quotation**
>
> 'the evil assumption — that *all* Negroes lie, that *all* Negroes are basically immoral beings, that *all* Negro men are not to be trusted around our women'
>
> (Atticus, Chapter 20)

Grade C essay

Scout thinks 'there's just one kind of folks. Folks' because she is a child and is not prejudiced. *To Kill a Mockingbird* is about racism and other forms of prejudice like community prejudice against misfits such as Boo Radley and Dolphus Raymond. Women are not equal yet either, [1] so they are not allowed on juries. **(AO4)** Aunt Alexandra thinks the Cunninghams are 'trash' because they are poor and cannot read and write. There is prejudice in favour of white people, even someone like Bob Ewell who drinks and knocks his daughter about. [2] **(AO1, AO4)**

1 Poorly expressed
2 Loose introduction; colloquialisms

Tom Robinson is acused [3] of raping Mayella Ewell but he never done it. [4] He only gets a sort-of [5] fair trial because Atticus is his lawyer. Mr Gilmer, who's on the other side, [5] just goes along with the prejudices of the jury. He sneers at Tom for doing stuff [5] for Mayella. He says 'I felt right sorry for her, she seemed to try more'n the rest of 'em — .' Mr Gilmer pounces on this. **(AO2)** In this community, a black man is not serposed [6] to feel sympathy for a white woman. **(AO1)** When Dill cries because this upsets him, Harper Lee is showing us that Mr Gilmer is immoral **(AO1)** although he should know better, being a lawyer like Atticus. For Tom, it's a tragedy.

3 Spelling mistake
4 Colloquialism and poor grammar
5 Colloquialism
6 Spelling mistake

Prejudice in the courtroom is not just against blacks. It also works in favour of Bob Ewell because he is white. Tom is a good man with a wife and children but he is black. **(AO4)** Bob Ewell is bad. He is violent and his children are filthy (Burris with head lice at school, for example). **(AO1)** He spends his dole money on booze [7] and probably sexually abuses Mayella ('She says what her papa do to her don't count'). But Ewell is white, so they think he is better than Tom. [8] **(AO4)**

7 Colloquialism
8 Argument not well structured

Lee reminds us that sometimes racial prejudice works both ways. **(AO1)** When Lula rounds on Calpurnia for bringing 'white chillun' to First Purchase Church, we feel a bit sorry for her. Harper Lee means that if you treat a group of people like rubbish, some of them will argue back. The incident helps to make *To Kill a Mockingbird* a balanced novel. **(AO1)**

There is also prejudice against Boo Radley. **(AO1)** He does not go out and people talk about him. For people like the gossipy Miss Stephanie Crawford, he is wicked or frightning, [9] so the children hear this and think it is true. That is why they play games about Boo and try to make him come out. But at the end we find out he is really harmless and quiet — just a bit simple. [10] **(AO1)** Harper Lee means that you should not believe everything people say. **(AO2)**

Aunt Alexandra upsets Scout by saying the Cunninghams are 'trash'. 'But they're not our kind of folks,' she says. Is she telling Scout something sensible or is Harper Lee against class prejudice too? **(AO2)** Aunt Alexandra's point is that 'Finch women aren't interested in that sort of people.' She does not want Scout mixing with them. Then Jem wonders why, if people are 'all alike, do they go out of their way to despise each other?' and tries to explain to Scout. **(AO2)**

Only men could be on juries in the Southern states in the 1930s. Scout asks Atticus why 'people like us and Miss Maudie' do not sit on juries. **(AO4)** Even Atticus cannot resist having a dig [11] about women interupting. [12] He also thinks the idea is to 'protect' women from hearing horrible things in court. But it is not fair that cases are heard by people who know each other because they meet down the shops and other business. **(AO1)** They cannot help having prejudice about each other. [13] Prejudice is a big theme in *To Kill a Mockingbird*. Harper Lee does not like it as she shows in her novel. [14] She makes characters say and do things to make her meaning clear. [15]

Overall this essay only gets enough marks for a C grade because, although it covers AO1, AO2 and AO4 in reasonable depth, it is not well structured and the expression is often inappropriate and sloppy.

Grade A* essay

Prejudice means pre-judgement or making up your mind about something because of a preconceived view and without looking open-mindedly at the evidence. That is exactly what the jury does at the trial of Tom Robinson. **(AO1)** Harper Lee who, like Scout, believes on the whole 'there's just one kind of folks. Folks' also makes us think, as we read *To Kill a Mockingbird,* about other forms of prejudice. These include black prejudice against white people, community prejudice against misfits such as Boo Radley and Dolphus Raymond, prejudice against women who talk too much and who are not permitted to sit on juries, class prejudice by someone like Aunt Alexandra who regards, say, the Cunninghams as 'trash' because they are poor and illiterate and, perhaps most interestingly, prejudice in favour of white people — even when someone is as dangerous as the lying, lazy Bob Ewell. [1] **(AO4)**

Tom Robinson, wrongfully accused of raping Mayella Ewell, only gets a relatively fair hearing because Atticus does everything he can to bring out the truth clearly

9 Spelling mistake
10 Colloquialism

11 Colloquialism
12 Spelling mistake
13 Poorly expressed
14 Not enough focus on how Lee makes her own views clear
15 Conclusion does not add anything

1 Strong introduction

in court. His opponent, prosecuting counsel Mr Gilmer, just plays to the prejudices of the jury and most of the white onlookers in court. He ridicules Tom's neighbourly habit of doing chores for Mayella. 'I was just tryin' to help her out,' Tom says, and then: 'I felt right sorry for her, she seemed to try more'n the rest of 'em —' **(AO1)**

Mr Gilmer pounces on this and Scout tells us, 'Below us, nobody liked Tom Robinson's answer.' The prejudices of this community are such that it is simply not acceptable for a black man to feel sympathy for a white woman. **(AO4)** Shortly after this, Dill begins to weep, moved by the dreadful injustice of it. Scout takes him out of court and we sense that this is Harper Lee's way of stressing that Gilmer, an educated white man, has casually condemned the innocent 'mockingbird' in the dock because that is what the segregated society of 1930s Alabama expects and requires. **(AO2, AO4)** When the jury finds Tom guilty — after longer deliberations than usual, which is some progress — we see the reactions of the children. Jem weeps and the black community is dignified and grateful. Atticus is exhausted. Harper Lee presents all the initial reaction to the verdict through the losers and so makes us aware that this is a true tragedy. **(AO1, AO2)**

Prejudice in the courtroom is not just against Tom Robinson because he is black. It also works in favour of Bob Ewell because he is white. **(AO1)** Harper Lee makes her feelings clear here because the characters she has created are extreme examples of good and bad. **(AO2)** Tom is a respectable, hard-working family man with a wife and three children but he is black. Bob Ewell is the violent father of seven filthy, neglected children (Burris with head lice who disrupts school, for example), who spends his welfare cheque on drink and probably sexually abuses Mayella ('She says what her papa do to her don't count,' Tom tells the court about Mayella's attempt to seduce him) — but Ewell is white. [2] As Scout sums it up for Harper Lee, 'in the secret courts of men's hearts Atticus had no case. Tom was a dead man the minute Mayella Ewell opened her mouth and screamed.' **(AO2)**

2 Uses evidence well

Only once in the novel does Lee remind us that sometimes racial prejudice works both ways. When Lula rounds on Calpurnia for bringing 'white chillun' to First Purchase Church, we feel a shred of sympathy for her although she is overridden by Calpurnia and Reverend Sykes. **(AO1, AO2, AO4)** Harper Lee is showing us that if you treat a group of people as underlings, even though in law they are supposed to have equality, some of them will try to turn the tables and that is understandable. The incident helps to make *To Kill a Mockingbird* a balanced novel. [3] **(AO1)**

3 Sustained argument reviews several sorts of prejudice

Another major form of prejudice in the novel works against Boo Radley because he is a recluse and there are rumours about him. [4] **(AO1)** For people like the gossip-loving Miss Stephanie Crawford, he must therefore be wicked or frightening. The children, not yet old enough to know better, take this idea and play with it at the

4 Sustained argument reviews several sorts of prejudice

beginning of the novel. By revealing the real Boo Radley as harmless, gentle, shy and damaged to Scout and to the reader at the end of the novel, Harper Lee shows us that most prejudices are based on falsehood. **(AO2)**

5 Sustained argument reviews several sorts of prejudice

She does the same thing in a more minor way with Dolphus Raymond. **5** Everyone thinks he's 'in the clutches of whiskey'. In fact, outside the courthouse during the trial, Scout and Dill discover for themselves that the drink he carries around with him is nothing stronger than Coca-Cola. Lee's message is surely to examine the evidence before you make a judgement. **(AO1, AO2)**

Aunt Alexandra upsets Scout by condemning the Cunninghams as 'trash' and refusing to allow Scout to invite Walter to the house. **(AO1)** 'But they're not our kind of folks,' she says, explaining that 'you can scrub Walter Cunningham till he shines, you can put him in shoes and a new suit, but he'll never be like Jem'. Is she telling Scout something that is actually reasonable or is Harper Lee condemning class prejudice too? **6** After all, Atticus sat at the table with Walter a year or two earlier when Jem invited him to lunch on Scout's first day at school. He talked to him courteously and Calpurnia insisted that Scout did too. Aunt Alexandra's point is that 'Finch women aren't interested in that sort of people', so she does not want Scout mixing with them. Then Harper Lee has Jem who wonders why, if people are 'all alike, they go out of their way to despise each other?' trying to explain it to Scout. **(AO2)**

6 Sustained argument reviews several sorts of prejudice

Juries in the Southern states of the 1930s were all male — to Scout's indignation. **(AO4)** In a conversation with Atticus, intended to draw the reader's attention to this prejudice **(AO2)**, which was over by the time the novel was published in 1960, Scout asks why 'people like us and Miss Maudie' do not sit on juries. Even Atticus cannot resist a quip about women interrupting. More seriously, he guesses (without condemnation) that the idea is to 'protect' women from sordid cases. Through his explanation to the children about small-town life — everyone knowing everyone else, shopping, money and local interests — we realise that a case is being made against the injustice of people being tried by juries who are known to them and therefore prejudiced in some way. **(AO4)**

Prejudice and attitudes to it is a major theme in *To Kill a Mockingbird*, which Harper Lee explores from a range of angles. Maycomb is an insular society, 'a tired old town' steeped in racial prejudice and its 'caste system'. **(AO1)** Apart from the possible exception of needing to be realistic about class differences, the author seems to be arguing strongly against it and makes her feelings clear through Scout's observations and her reports of what other characters say and do. **(AO2)**

The essay is outstandingly well expressed, with accurate punctuation and spelling. It weaves in many short, well-used quotations and addresses AO1, AO2 and AO4 throughout.

Question 3 (higher and foundation tier: OCR, WJEC, AQA, Edexcel or CCEA)

Read from 'Miss Caroline began the day by reading' to 'You can have a seat now' (Chapter 2, starting about one page in from the beginning of the chapter).

Higher tier: How does Lee use the details in this passage to show the different cultures of Miss Caroline and the children? How does Lee present Scout's education in the novel as a whole?

Foundation tier: How does Lee use the details in this passage to show the different cultures of Miss Caroline and the children? How does Lee present Scout's education in the novel as a whole?

Write about:
- what Miss Caroline says and does in the classroom
- the children's reaction to her
- ways in which Scout is educated at school and at home and by what happens in the community
- methods Lee uses to show Scout's education

Note: this is the same question. There is simply more guidance for the foundation tier. That is why the grade C sample essay below could have been written by someone entered for either tier.

Grade A* essay (higher tier)

Miss Caroline's main problem is that she has no understanding of, or respect for, anything the children already know or can do. Lee presents the misunderstanding humorously but actually it is rather a sad reflection on her narrow 1930s teacher training and lack of experience. [1] **(AO4)**

1 Clear, well-expressed introduction

Miss Caroline, who is very young and in her first teaching job, starts her first day with Scout's class by reading aloud a sentimental and anthropomorphic [2] story about cats. It might have appealed to middle class children in a prosperous New York suburb **(AO4)** but it makes Maycomb's first grade in their denim shirts and flour sacks wriggle 'like a bucketful of Catawba worms' — a nice simile which every child in the class would have understood but Miss Caroline would not — which is an interesting reflection on the education they already have but which their teacher lacks. **(AO2, AO4)** The farm children of Maycomb, as Lee has the adult Scout remark with hindsight and irony, 'were immune to imaginative literature'. Lee makes us smile, too, at Miss Caroline's unawareness of the unsuitability of the story. 'Oh, my, wasn't that nice?' she says imperviously when she has finished. **(AO1, AO2, AO4)**

2 Accurate use of vocabulary

Her next gaffe [3] is to write letters on the blackboard and ask the children if they know what they are. Here the humour lies in the terseness of the adult Scout's one-sentence paragraph comment. 'Everybody did; most of the first grade had failed it last year.' **(AO2)** Miss Caroline seems not to realise that in the USA it is (or was) quite usual for a child to repeat a school year — often several times — because he or she hasn't reached the required standard. In the Maycomb of *To Kill a Mockingbird* school attendance of many children is poor (as the incident with Burris Ewell elsewhere in this chapter shows), usually because they are needed as labourers on the family land. Without child labour, in the financially troubled 1930s, some of these families would have starved. **(AO4)** One of the results, of course, is that the children do not progress in school work and many will remain unable to read and write. Presumably Bob Ewell, for example, had very little schooling. There is a question mark over whether or not he is literate at the trial, later in the novel. [4]

Scout, on the other hand, can already read although she is younger than many of the children repeating first grade and this is her first day at school. She has learned to read effortlessly and by absorption at home with some basic help from Calpurnia. 'Reading was something that just came to me' she says, elsewhere in the novel. **(AO1)** Miss Caroline, who has been introduced to Scout socially in the town before school starts, asks Scout a question because she knows her name and is then disconcerted because Scout reads all the letters written on the board. The teacher then asks her to read aloud from a class reader and from the local newspaper and discovers 'with more than faint distaste' **(AO1)** that she is literate. More irony follows **(AO2)** as Miss Caroline says that her father must not teach her anymore because it would interfere with her reading. [5] Scout replies, in amazement, that 'Atticus aint got time to teach me anything' but the reader already knows **(AO1)** that Scout is an intelligent, thinking, knowledgeable child who has learned almost everything she knows directly (or indirectly via Jem) from Atticus and, although much of her learning during the next two years comes through the community, Atticus remains the main guiding force who interprets and guides her learning — sometimes very unobtrusively. The 'damage' that Miss Caroline says Atticus has done to Scout's education is clearly more to do with Miss Caroline's feeling uneasy at having a bright child to teach than with Scout's needs. **(AO1)**

Although Lee shows us that Scout's first day at school is educationally unpromising ('twelve years of unrelieved boredom' ahead?) she learns a lot through the things which happen in the rest of the novel — and, as Atticus points out that evening [6] she has anyway learned several things from a day with Miss Caroline even if it wasn't what the teacher intended. **(AO1)** For example Scout (and Jem and Dill) gradually learn what is really 'different' about Boo Radley. [7] Lee shows us them playing, noticing things, speculating and talking to adults. Boo isn't the half crazed figure of fun the children create in the One Man's Family games. Instead, as she eventually realises, he is a timid, delicate, pale man with a nervous twitch capable of single minded, selfless action for others — rescuing the children from Bob Ewell. **(AO1)** She has to find this out for herself. Had she listened to the wise Miss Maudie and to Atticus she might have known the truth about Boo earlier. **(AO2)**

From the many possible examples of Scout's wider education and the way Lee presents it, I will mention just two more. [8] Lee sends Scout and Jem to Calpurnia's church **(AO2)** so that we can see them learning and learn with them. Among other things, Scout learns that Calpurnia has two speech modes and why. She realises that most of Maycomb's black population is illiterate because they have had no schooling — which is why they have to sing their hymns line by line, led by Calpurnia's son Zeebo, taught to read by his mother. **(AO1)** Then there's the realisation that black people can be just as hostile to whites as the other way round when Lula tells Calpurnia that 'white chillun' are not welcome at the church. **(AO1)** She also learns that Tom's wife Helen is in dire need with her husband in prison and nobody willing to employ her and watches as the very poor people at the church rally round and donate the money Reverend Sykes says is required. **(AO2)**

> 8 Clear signposting within essay

Second, Lee contrives a way of getting Scout (with Jem and Dill) to Tom Robinson's trial, the novel's central event. **(AO2)** This is so that the reader can be given an eyewitness account of it **(AO2)** and so that Scout and we can learn. Jem leads her to believe that justice will prevail and Atticus will win Tom's case, although Atticus knows otherwise. She also learns about justice, the horror of Mayella Ewell's life, the human decency of Tom Robinson, the unorthodox but effective way in which Judge Taylor manages his court, the attitude of the local white people and the dignity of the black community among whom the children sit. **(AO4)** Lee presents all this by placing Scout, initially against orders from Atticus and Aunt Alexandra, at the heart of the action and showing us what happens through Scout's eyes, which includes the tension when the children are outside the courtroom and we, like them, long to know what's going on. **(AO2)**

By the end of the novel over two years have passed during which Lee has shown us Scout growing up **(AO2)** and we see that her education is proceeding well — partly in school (Miss Caroline would have been her teacher for only one year) **(AO4)** but crucially also in the community through her family and fellow Maycomb inhabitants. Some of the learning — the discussions with Atticus, Uncle Jack and Miss Maudie, for instance — is deliberate and almost formal but much of it simply happens because of what is going on around Scout.

This is an impeccably structured and beautifully written essay which covers all three AOs fully. It is impressively detailed and includes a lot of analytical comment and interpretation.

Grade *booster*

Make a list of the main differences between a grade C answer and an A* answer. Think about how, using the advice given here, you can improve your own written answers.

Grade C essay (higher and foundation tier)

1 Colloquialism
2 Spelling error

Miss Caroline doesn't understand that the children already know stuff [1] and that they come from a different background to her. This passage is quite funny — Lee wants us to laugh at the ignorent [2] teacher. **(AO2)**

3 Colloquialisms

Miss Caroline read them a babyish story about cats. It might have been OK [3] for her when she was a kid [3] but it makes Maycomb's first grade fidget like 'a bucketful of Catawba worms' (she wouldn't have known what they were). The farm children of Maycomb, as Scout says looking back, didn't get imaginative literature but Miss Caroline doesn't seem to realise. **(AO4)**

4 Colloquialisms
5 Spelling error

Then, stupidly, she writes letters on the blackboard and asks the children if they know what they are. Miss Caroline doesn't seem to know that in the USA kids [4] often have to stay down a year at school if they don't pass there [5] tests — although I reckon [4] she should if she's a teacher and been to college. In *To Kill a Mockingbird* many kids [4] (like the Ewells) don't go to school much because they have to help their parents at home with growing stuff. So they can't pass school tests. **(AO4)**

6 Spelling error

Scout can already read although she's only 6. She has learned at home with a bit of help from Calprunia. [6] She says 'Reading was something that just came to me.' Miss Caroline asks Scout a question because she knows her name and is then cross because Scout reads all the letters written on the board. She also reads aloud from a class reader and a newspaper to show that she can read. **(AO1)**

7 Colloquialisms

Miss Caroline says that her father must not teach her anymore because it would interfere with her reading — and that's funny because she can already read so it wouldn't make no difference what her dad [7] did. Scout says 'Atticus ain't got time to teach me anything' and that's funny too because Lee shows Scout is bright and has learned loads [7] from Atticus (and Jem). Even when other people are showing her things and teaching her she still gets help from Atticus. **(AO1)** I reckon [7] Miss Caroline just doesn't like having a child to teach who's cleverer than her. **(AO1)**

8 Useful way of widening essay out from focusing on the passage to the rest of the novel

Although Lee shows us that Scout's first day at school is not much good (she thinks she's got to put up with 'twelve years of unrelieved boredom') she learns a lot in other ways later. [8] For example Scout (and the boys) gradually learn what's wrong about Boo Radley. Lee shows us them **(AO2)** playing about, noticing things, making up stories and asking grown ups. Boo isn't the nutty, scary man the children make up in the One Man's Family games. In the end Scout finds out he's just a nervous, shy sort but he's kind and not selfish. He rescues the children from Bob Ewell. **(AO1)** Scout would have known this already if she'd listened to Miss Maudie and Atticus.

9 Poor English. 'Examples' or 'episodes' would be better

I will write about just two more times [9] when Scout gets educated in the rest of the book and how Lee presents it.

Scout and Jem go to Calprunia's [10] church. Scout learns that Calprunia [10] has two different ways of speaking. She realises that most of Maycomb's blacks don't go to school and can't read. Then she's suprised [10] that black people can hate whites as well when Lula tells Calprunia [10] that 'white chillun' **(AO2)** should be in their own place. She also learns that Tom's wife Helen needs money so the church people collect it although there [10] ever so poor. Lee puts the church visit in purposely so that we get [11] all this. **(AO1, AO2)**

Second, Lee makes Scout (with Jem and Dill) be at Tom Robinson's trial. This is so she can tell the reader about it. **(AO2)** But she learns a lot of stuff [12] too. Jem tells her Atticus will win Tom's case but he doesn't. She also learns about write [13] and wrong, the horrible life Mayella Ewell has and how nice [14] Tom Robinson is. She's gobsmacked [12] at how Judge Taylor runs the court and she learns a lot about what local white people are really like. She also sees that the black people are sort of [12] better. **(AO1)** Lee tells the story that Scout (Atticus and Aunt Alexandra have said no) is in the middle of where it's all happening so it's exciting too. **(AO2)**

At the end of the book Scout is over two years older and she has learned a lot so she's getting her education in different ways. Atticus (and Uncle Jack and Miss Maudie) teach and tell her things on purpose but a lot of her learning just happens because of the stuff [15] that's going on. [16]

10 Spelling error

11 Colloquialism

12 Colloquialisms
13 Spelling error
14 Imprecise vocabulary

15 Colloquialism
16 Conclusion rounds off essay satisfactorily

This essay is reasonably well structured and answers the question. It moves from the passage to the rest of the novel and covers the three AOs. It lacks detail, however, and the expression is often inappropriate. Although the spelling errors do not prevent the examiner from understanding the argument there are too many of them.

Grade E essay (foundation tier)

Miss Caroline is a young teecher. [1] The children don't like her cats story and they mess about. She don't [2] understand them because there [1] different to her. They are like worms in a bucket. **(AO1)**

When she puts letters on the board Scout (story teller) can read them. She as [2] not been to school before but she has been learned [2] to read at home by her dad and by the black cook Calprunia.[1] Some of the other kids [4] have been to school loads of times [4] before but they keep failing there [1] tests because they have days off to help there [1] mums and dads with growing stuff. [4] **(AO4)** Scout can read so good [2] that she reads to the teecher [1] from a newspaper and another thing as well. **(AO1)** She gets told off but nowadays a teecher [1] would say it was good if a little kid [4] could read like a grown up. **(AO4)**

Then Miss Caroline says that her father — he's called Atticus and Scout never says Dad or Daddy — must not teech [1] her anymore because he don't [2] know how to

1 Spelling errors including names
2 Errors in English
3 Names carelessly remembered
4 Colloquialism or inappropriate English

teech [1] and it will stop her learning and reading. But in the rest of the book Atticus does teech [1] Scout stuff alot. [2] **(AO1)**

Scout (and the boys) learn more about Boo Radley. They get told [4] things by a woman neighbour (I can't remember her name) and by Atticus. The kids think he is a nutter and scary. [4] But at the end he's just a quiet man. And he stops Scout and her brother being killed. **(AO1)**

Scout goes to a black people's church with the cook and learns stuff [4] there about black people so it's a kind of education for her. None of em [1] can read and Caprunia [1] speaks funny. [4] Scout sees them collecting money for a poor woman (her husband's serposed [1] to have raped a white girl) although they ain't [2] got much themselves. **(AO1, AO4)**

At the trial (Tim Robertson) [3] the kids [4] think he will get off. [4] But the jury says he did it. Scout and the boys are in court **(AO2)** so she learns stuff [4] — sort of like [4] being in school. She finds out that trials are'nt [1] always fair. And she hears what a horrible life Manilla [3] Ewell has. It's good [4] that the kids [4] are there so Scout can say what happens. **(AO2)**

Grade *booster*

What is the main difference between a grade C and a grade E answer? Think about how, using the advice given here, you can improve your answers.

This essay is very short but it shows some knowledge and understanding both of the passage and the rest of the novel. There is much AO1 (it explains what happens), some AO4 (the context) but little AO2 (analysis of how Harper Lee tells her story and why). It is, however, poorly expressed with a lot of inappropriate language and faulty spelling. There is some structure in that it starts by discussing the passage before moving on to the rest of the novel.

How to get an A* grade

To get an A* grade, you must:

- answer the question fully or do exactly what the task asks you to do
- construct a clear argument or line of reasoning
- make good use of frequent short quotations within your sentences
- shape your answer by planning it with an introduction and a conclusion
- express your ideas in good English
- write clearly, with precision and in an appropriate tone
- spell accurately

Key quotation

'every lawyer gets at least one case in his lifetime that affects him personally. This one's mine, I guess'

(Atticus, Chapter 9)

Review your learning

1 What is meant by 'textual evidence'?

2 What is the main difference between a higher-tier question and a foundation-tier question?

3 What are the three main things that GCSE questions on *To Kill a Mockingbird* are likely to focus on?

4 How will you set about devising an essay plan?

5 What might you include in:

   a an essay introduction?

   b an essay conclusion?

 More interactive questions and answers online.

Answers

Answers to 'Review your learning' questions.

Context (page 11)

1 She was born in Monroeville, Alabama in 1926, the youngest of four children. Their father was a lawyer.
2 The Northerners banned slavery. The Southern states, including Alabama, wanted it to continue, so they tried to break away from the North to form the Confederate States. The Northerners would not allow this.
3 Martin Luther King Junior
4 Southern novels tend to be regional and to present a strong sense of place. They also convey a feeling of loneliness and isolation. They show a pride in tradition but criticise racial prejudice. Southern novels also often present guilt.
5 The answer is up to you, but it could include Lee's desire to expose the evil of prejudice in all its forms and to try to explain its origins.
6 The answer requires an opinion, but some of the novel's appeal almost certainly lies in the following: its strong characterisation and the appeal of its characters; its dry humour; good storytelling, with strong elements of suspense and mystery; its appeal to the better side of human nature.

Plot and structure (page 29)

1 Miss Maudie
2 a Jimmy
  b Francis
3 Mr Link Deas
4 Reverend Sykes makes the black people in the gallery stand up to show respect for Atticus as he leaves the court at the end of the trial.
5 This is a matter of personal interpretation. However, be aware that the novel is in two parts. In Part Two, Jem is bordering on adolescence and is beginning to grow apart from Scout. Significant events include:
  ● the children's attempts to make Boo Radley come out, and the presents he leaves them in the hollow tree, which stop when his brother Nathan fills in the hole

- Miss Maudie's house burning down
- Atticus shooting the rabid dog, which influences the children's view of him (especially Jem's)
- Jem having to read to Mrs Dubose
- Aunt Alexandra coming to stay
- the trial and death of Tom Robinson
- Bob Ewell's attack on the children
- Scout finally meeting Boo Radley

6 This question has no single correct answer. However, you could argue for either the trial's 'guilty' verdict or the attack on the children by Bob Ewell as being the climax.

Characterisation (page 43)

1 Miss Maudie (of Atticus)
2 Boo Radley
3 Cecil Jacobs, Francis, Mrs Dubose
4 She shows the characters speaking, acting and responding. She allows us to share Scout's responses at first hand. If Scout is surprised, puzzled or delighted, so are we. Lee also uses humour.
5 This is a matter of opinion, but remember that Scout is the narrator as well as being a major character. On the other hand, there is a great deal of close focus on Atticus and Jem.

Themes (page 52)

1 An idea, or set of ideas, threaded through a piece of writing
2 Racism, family, mockingbirds, courage and growing up
3 Tom Robinson and Boo Radley
4 Moral courage
5 The suffering caused by racist ignorance
6 This could be any of the children, but Jem is a strong contender.

Style (page 59)

1 First-person narrative
2 The first-person narrator can describe at first hand only things that he or she has personally witnessed. Scout cannot be present at every event in the novel. Lee gets around this by having other characters report events to Scout.
3 The racism that fuels the novel's two central events (the rape trial and Ewell's attack on the children) was a feature of the Southern states.

A feature of the small-town setting is that everyone knows everyone else and can comment on them.

4 ● To establish character. Calpurnia's 'hand was as wide as a bed slat and twice as hard'. Mayella's nervousness is stressed by Scout's description of her as 'a steady-eyed cat with a twitchy tail' (Chapter 18).

● To convey feeling, as in Scout's distaste for Mrs Dubose: 'Her face was the colour of a dirty pillowcase, and the corners of her mouth glistened with wet, which inched like a glacier down the deep grooves enclosing her chin' (Chapter 11).

● To evoke a sense of place. An example is the Ewell's home being like 'the playhouse of an insane child' (Chapter 17).

● Linked to symbolism, as in the mockingbird of the title, a metaphor for innocence and vulnerability.

5 Uncle Jack is an educated man living in the North. Mr Cunningham is a poor, uneducated farmer from the South. 'Her use of invective leaves nothing to the imagination' (Uncle Jack, Chapter 9). 'It was obstreperous, disorderly and abusive' (Uncle Jack, Chapter 9). 'Mr Finch, I don't know when I'll ever be able to pay you' (Mr Cunningham, Chapter 2). 'I'll tell him you said hey, little lady' (Mr Cunningham, Chapter 15).

Sample essays (page 89)

1 Textual evidence is the use of quotations, or references, to events or descriptions from the novel to back up your answers.

2 Foundation-tier questions have bullet points to help you construct an answer; higher-tier questions do not.

3 Plot, character and theme

4 Work out what you think the question is asking to you to do. Highlight key words in the question. Jot down your main ideas and number them in order.

5 a How you are going to tackle the question, your interpretation of the question or a comment on something in it

b A summary of your arguments, or a paragraph drawing them together in a new way — a new point you have held back for the ending